NO-H-IN SNAKE

Music Theory
FOR CHILDREN

by MICHIKO YURKO

© Copyright MCMLXXIX by Alfred Publishing Co., Inc.

Published by Alfred Publishing Co., Inc.
15335 Morrison Street, Sherman Oaks, CA 91403

Copyright © 1979 by Michiko Yurko
Sole selling agent Alfred Publishing Co., Inc.

Printed in the United States of America

All rights reserved.
No part of this book shall be reproduced
or transmitted in any form or by
any means, electronic or mechanical
including photocopying, recording, or by
any information or retrieval system
without written permission of the Publisher.

Library of Congress Cataloging in Publication Data

Yurko, Michiko, 1951–
No-H-in snake.

Includes index.
1. Music—Instruction and study—Juvenile.
2. Music—Theory, Elementary. I. Title.
MT1.Y87   372.8'72   70-9154
ISBN 0-88284-092-4

Editor, SANDY FELDSTEIN
Interior designer, MARYLYNN CONTE
Cover design, WILLIAM CONTE
Line drawings, MARYLYNN CONTE based on
illustrations by MICHIKO YURKO

Contents

*To my husband, Richard, for his love,
understanding and patience
during the preparation
of this book.*

Acknowledgments

I wish to express deep gratitude to Dr. Shinichi Suzuki. He envisioned a splendid approach to educating children, then shared his discovery with the world. He showed us that each child has natural abilities which can be developed to achieve excellence and with them a noble mind and a high sense of values. Together child and adult seek not only music but love, self-discipline, truth and high character.

Special *love* and appreciation is extended to my mother, Mary Fujii Henshall for her enthusiasm, encouragement and advice not only during the preparation of this book, but throughout my life.

Warmest thanks to Richard for the care he took with the photographs. I am grateful to Arthur Montzka for his outstanding photographs found throughout the book.

Michiko Yurko

Preface

I'd like to take a moment to speak briefly about the teaching ideas of Dr. Shinichi Suzuki of Matsumoto, Japan. He feels that talent is not an inborn ability. Through the child's own environment, he can learn great things; his potential is absolutely unlimited.

Suzuki feels that children everywhere show remarkable ability by learning to speak their own complex languages. More than this, they learn to speak fluently, with great ease, and a high level of proficiency. It is later that they learn to interpret the written symbols which represent speech so they might learn to read and write. He believes this same approach can be applied to learning music. And what a happy experience it can be.

Ideally, children listen to good music from birth. Around the age of two or three the children come together to watch their mothers taking lessons with a well-trained Suzuki teacher. They play the piano, special 1/16 size violins, or miniature cellos. By this time the music they are hearing daily is focused on the music they will be learning. Soon the child begins his own lessons with the mother (or father) continuing as an important part of the lesson so she might be an effective teacher at home.

While my students are developing proper playing techniques, good tone, evenness of tempo, and musical sensitivity, I feel they can begin to learn the basic fundamentals of music notation. Not wanting to interfere with the procedures Dr. Suzuki has developed, I teach this at a time other than the lesson. These concepts can be introduced slowly since there is no hurry to learn them in order to play pieces on their instrument. This allows for a thorough, complete study without a need to rush over details. When I feel it is time to begin reading music, the child will feel free to concentrate on the process of reading since he is comfortable with the fundamentals of theory.

Of course, children can learn to read music without knowing the principles of theory. It wasn't until college that I realized tonic wasn't only something you put on your hair or drank at a party. When faced with the multiple choice question of what side of the note a sharp was written during a theory placement exam I actually hesitated. I'd learned concertos and sonatas by reading music, but never having had to write it, I realized I hardly knew how to write out the simplest of tunes. And dictation—after learning this wasn't only for secretaries, I was thrilled to get a five-note pattern. But, my brain and ears made no connection when I first heard more complex melodies and harmonies. How difficult it was because I learned these concepts when I was eighteen rather than eight, or even three or four.

So I decided not to take it for granted that my students would learn enough theory while they learned to read music. While I wanted them to learn solid concepts I didn't want it to be a boring event, so I began using games and an assortment of brightly colored materials. You can see what evolved.

In the past few years I have been in contact with teachers across the country who, after observing my classes at Suzuki Institutes or taking a teacher-training workshop, began to incorporate the theory games into their teaching. Many use these ideas in their general music programs in the schools. I have heard from enthusiastic teachers who use the games with their church choirs. Because the ideas in this book are not limited to use with Suzuki students, I have refrained from specific references to the Suzuki literature. I hope this will give teachers greater flexibility and freedom to use the games to enhance their own programs.

To many of you who have been waiting patiently for this book to appear, I have many kind thoughts. Each time I've rewritten this book, I've tried to make it more concise and clearer. I've listened to your questions and hope I've answered many of them. I've included hundreds of drawings and photos to reinforce the text so that a glance might be all you need to refresh your memory about a certain game you want to play.

Although I've attempted to explain each step by using direct instructions, this doesn't mean it's the only way to do it. I'm a person of change. If my students understand what I'm teaching them, I'm pleased. If they don't, I remake the game sequence so they do understand.

I'd like to share one re-occurring comment from teachers who have been using my ideas: "It's so easy and fun to teach. The children just love it."

Best wishes!

Michiko Yurko

There are patterns to make all the materials used to play the games and early steps are being taken to have some things ready-made. Information is available from:

> MUSIC 19
> P.O. Box 2431
> Rockville, Maryland 20852

SUGGESTED READING FOR INFORMATION ABOUT THE SUZUKI APPROACH

Nurtured by Love: A New Approach to Education by Shinichi Suzuki
The Suzuki Violinist: A Guide for Teachers and Parents by William Starr
Ability from Age Zero by Shinichi Suzuki
The Suzuki Concept: An Introduction to a Successful Method for Early Music Education
    edited by Elizabeth Mills and Sister Therese Cecile Murphy

further information can be obtained by writing to:

> THE SUZUKI ASSOCIATION OF THE AMERICAS, INC.
> The Batterson Building
> P.O. Box 354
> Muscatine, Iowa 52761

NO-H-IN SNAKE

Music Theory

FOR CHILDREN

1
Teaching Music Theory to Children

Music theory is a logical and lovely language, as basic to musicianship as the sun is to the unfolding of a beautiful flower. It's to a young child's advantage to receive a foundation for music theory from the beginning of his musical study, and as he progresses to learn it thoroughly and correctly.

So here's Henry, eager to learn how to read music. He's seen Teacher and Mother reading from the music book and he wants to try too. He's curious about the different shapes and lines they've been talking about.

The wise teacher will strive to channel this interest into effective learning. But how much should she tell him? There's so much to learn.

Let's say his teacher places a music book in front of Henry and begins an excellent discourse on note reading. Soon a small frown appears on his face. After a few moments any curiosity he had is replaced by an exploring finger on the keys or reaching to see if perhaps there's another picture on the next page.

What happened to that initial curiosity? Did she try to teach him too much? Precisely. Besides the staff, his book probably contained pictures to attract (but most likely distract) his attention and paragraphs of words for his teacher to read to him. It was just too much for Henry to look at and listen to at once.

Each page of music is a collection of a multitude of concepts—each one essential in translating the written idea into beautiful sound. It's expecting a lot of a child to be able to interpret very much of this in the beginning. An alternative is to divide each of these important musical concepts into small steps that the child can handle at his own pace. Why not begin by using an idea with which he's already comfortable—the seven letters used in music: A, B, C, D, E, F, and G. Working with these familiar letters gives him that confidence necessary to begin on the road to reading music. "This isn't hard at all," he thinks, "I already know these letters!"

The steps can progress on to such activities as learning to recognize lines from spaces, spelling thirds, recognizing names of notes and how they relate to his instrument, reading rhythms and writing simple melodies all before he's asked to play from a page of music. By this time he's become comfortable with what music looks and sounds like.

With so many steps to cover, you ask, won't the child find this lengthy study of note reading boring or discouraging? Just having Mother and Teacher say it's important is hardly reason enough for him to like learning to read music.

The secret then is to let the child motivate himself—to take advantage of that initial curiosity. Let *him* discover about reading music. As unaware of your guidance as possible, help him to discover important concepts for himself.

To Illustrate

My young nephew was laboring over his math homework. He came across a puzzler and asked his father to listen. "Dad . . . 'A jet plane travels 500 miles an hour. If it took the plane six hours to fly from Washington, D.C. to San Diego, how many miles did it fly?' . . . It's just that I don't know if I should multiply or divide."

His Dad answered with authority, "Multiply."

Baffled and dubious, he asked, "Are you sure?"

"Of course I'm sure. That's the answer."

"Why wouldn't you divide, Dad?"

Ha! I thought. I can try out my theory about helping the child discover the answer for himself. Picking up a paper clip, I began.

"Brian, this paper clip is the plane—varoom! And this space between my fingers is 500 miles. The plane flies six hours, so the paper clip moves six times. Now to find the distance from Washington to San Diego, would you multiply or divide?"

"Easy! You'd multiply." And he went happily back to work, confident in *his* correct answer.

With his father's solution he was still in a fog; with the paper clip and the space between his fingers, he quickly saw the answer himself. Most important, he was beaming with confidence and eager to continue.

You can see that what he'd learned would stay with him because he was actively involved. He didn't just listen—he discovered and did it himself. How exciting to be challenged with something new and to suddenly see the light. Any child can figure out an answer if they aren't given too much to handle at once.

Therefore, the basis of this approach to learning music theory is to move in small steps, learning each one thoroughly before moving on to the next. Each of these small steps is learned through a progression of highly entertaining games which the child plays with teacher or mother, or with other children. Each game deals with one isolated aspect of music theory. By repeating each game again and again, at his delighted requests, the child commits this concept to memory with no effort outside of having a lot of fun.

These games have a tantalizing magic about them. In the excitement of playing, the children never quite realize that the games are designed so that everyone wins. Thus, the games are played with much suspense and excitement, with peals of laughter and clapping of hands. This fascination is of paramount importance.

This approach is completely child-oriented. Teachers and parents who have watched such theory classes, have remarked with wonder and enthusiasm that they've neven seen children having so much fun learning music theory. Classes of preschoolers can concentrate up to an hour, totally absorbed and so involved with creative thinking that they can come up with innovations that keep everyone on their toes.

How is it that everyone can have such a good time learning what's been labeled the dullest, hardest subject of music? The children are succeeding at what they're doing. And what could make a teacher happier?

Success creates in all of us that inner drive to continue learning and discovering. As a teacher, strive to ask a question or present a situation in such a manner that, first the child's thinking is stimulated, and second he can come up with the correct answer. Build upon this so there'll be the success of another correct response. And so a chain of small successes grows into the ultimate understanding.

Begin with an easy problem that will ellicit a logical answer. If a child is shy or unresponsive, quickly shift way back and begin building up to the original question.

There's no pat list of questions, for what may be easy for Steve may elude Diane. Lynne might remember that there's no H in our musical alphabet but you might have to remind Richard again and again.

Although this approach uses games as the vehicles to learning, there are no gimmicks, cute sayings or sugar-coated words to help the child memorize. Instead, he learns the real concepts with the real names and then commits them to memory through joyful repetition. It's the intellect that must be trained, the thought process that needs to be developed.

The games can begin shortly after the first lessons. As a Suzuki teacher, I prefer to keep the theory separate from the study of the instrument until the technical and musical skills are secure. Like two trees growing side by side, as they grow and mature their branches intertwine beautifully and eventually they're as one.

These theory games work just as effectively with students who are not studying by the Suzuki approach. You'll see how well they reinforce the instrumental study as they develop an understanding of music theory. The games have also proven a delight for children in general music programs. I even know of a group of senior citizens who used these games as part of an art and music appreciation class.

These games excite children of all ages. Since I often begin students at the tender age of three and four, many of the games are designed with them in mind. Obviously, if you're teaching an eleven-year-old, it'll be unnecessary for him to play some of the very early games. What he may cover in the first few sessions might take a four-year-old up to a year to learn.

Therefore, for best results, familiarize yourself with the games in sequence so that you can best adapt them to fit the needs of each child.

It's up to the teacher and parent to present the materials in such a way that the child meets with success each step of the way and has so much fun that he scarcely realizes what a valuable concept he's learned. He'll proceed with confidence and anticipation, eager to discover and learn more.

A.M.

CORNERSTONES

1. Assume that the child knows nothing but is brilliant and can learn anything.

2. What the child discovers for himself is what he'll remember.

3. If the child seems confused, it's not because he's slow, it's because the teacher is presenting the materials incorrectly.

4. Move in many small steps rather than one big step.

5. If the child meets with success each step along the way, he'll enjoy learning and want to discover more.

6. Never embarrass a child. If a mistake occurs, help him to learn how to correct it himself.

7. See that the child learns the concept first and then commits it to memory through repetition.

8. Review old games often so children can enjoy their progress.

9. Create an enjoyable learning environment so that the child is eager to learn.

10. The true objective of teaching should be the long term retention of the information, not how quickly it can be taught and memorized.

A.M.

2
Tips On Presenting the Materials

All Children Can Succeed.

During my years as a student I couldn't help but be aware of the different abilities of my classmates. There were those who always did well, those who rarely got things correct and a varying assortment of those in the middle. How discouraging it must have been for those who rarely succeeded. They probably needed more time to learn, but unfortunately, the classes weren't paced at their level of learning. Even though everyone didn't understand, on we went to new topics.

These students just seemed to get further and further behind. Somewhere along the way, they probably accepted their shortcomings and regretably formed a low opinion of their abilities. Hopefully, they'd find success later.

The reasons for this unbalanced learning situation have been explored in a great number of books and it's not my purpose here. Instead, I'd like to suggest guidelines in addition to the CORNERSTONES for helping each child to succeed, at least in their studies with music theory.

Obviously, there are advantages to teaching one subject to a small group of children; these advantages can be used to their full potential.

Teaching or Correcting?

There's a valuable concept that lies at the heart of Maria Montesorri's philosophies of education.

Teach *teaching*, not correcting. If the students make a mistake, don't correct them because if they could do it right, they would and when they can do it right, they will. They want to be right. If they make an error, make a note of it yourself and next time reteach it.

To Illustrate

A group of 4 and 5 year olds are playing 3-F: MUSIC BINGO for the first time. (Please read a description of the game on page 55.)

The teacher has previewed the game with them (3-E: PRE-BINGO) and feels confident about the children's ability to discriminate between high and low lines and spaces on the staff.

Each of the children has a bingo card and four bingo dots. As the teacher moves the bingo note to various lines and spaces on the one-staff board, the children place the bingo dots over the notes on their cards.

During the game the teacher hardly speaks but watches intently to see how well the children are matching the notes. He observes one little boy cover his lowest line note when the bingo note is on the top line.

Correcting the child in front of his peers, "Richard, not that note, this one on the *top* line. Put your bingo disc here," may not only embarrass him but confuse him as well.

It would be more effective for the teacher to make a mental note that Richard is confusing high and low notes. Before playing bingo the next time the teacher should go over the pre-bingo game with all the children and especially help Richard to understand up and down on the staff.

Any Testing?

If misused, the games described in this book could easily become mini-testing situations. Remember that they're not designed so that the children ever feel like they are being tested. Always help everyone to succeed. That's your responsibility.

To Illustrate

If you sense that a child can answer a question or name a note, allow him his moment to shine and let him speak up. However, if he pauses and a hint of doubt shows in his eyes, say the answer yourself, without quizzing him. After he repeats the answer, smile and tell him, "Good. You've got it."

Keeping Control.

Strive to keep on top of the situation at all times. Remain calm, friendly and let the children know exactly what type of behavior you expect. Encourage positive comments from them as well.

To Illustrate

"Let's do some dictation." I said one day.
"Oh. We'd rather make snakes." I heard them reply.
So we had a little chat about saying good things. I told them that my feelings were hurt if I thought they didn't like a certain game. They certainly understood about hurt feelings. We discussed being positive instead. I tried the opening statement again.
"Let's do some dictation." I saw smiles.
"Oh, dictation. Yea. We love it. Our favorite." They laughed.
The atmosphere continued to be pleasant the remainder of class.

Keep your directions short but clear and complete. If the children are confused about what they're to do they're more apt to lose interest and misbehave.

Help things to be happy. Humor is an indispensible tool in teaching. The children love a little joking around during class.

Imagine the following class situation. We're playing games where the children need to raise their hands if they know the answer to my question. Things are getting rowdy and it's hard to concentrate. I ask the children to put their hands on their knees. Once they know the answer they can gently fold their hands in their lap. Then I call on one child or go around the circle letting each child with clasped hands give the answer. It calms everyone down with no need for scolding.

Keep a notebook of what you do each week. It'll help you stay organized and know what to do in the next session.

Like your students. Take personal pleasure in their achievements. Show them how proud you are when they do something well. Even if they just tried to get the answer is reason enough to praise them. It's your kind words and smiles that'll encourage them to do even better.

Be sincere, praising something that isn't good is unfair to everyone. Look closely for there's always something good.

Above all, be honest with them. They'll respect you for that. If you goof up a game or forget an answer, smile and tell them. It won't hurt for them to see you make mistakes.

Organizing Theory Classes as a Private Teacher.

Experience has shown me that weekly theory classes of six to eight children not only provide the opportunity for good theory lessons every seven days but the chance for otherwise "private" music students to develop friendships among fellow students. Everything is much nicer when children can look forward to seeing their friends each week. The lesson becomes a pleasant, comfortable learning situation with the children relaxed and interested.

Dividing the children with consideration to age as well as ability is suggested. You can determine if your groupings are good if you find that:

1. The children feel comfortable together
2. They learn at about the same pace

In my present situation, children kindergarten and older, come for one hour theory class once a week in addition to their piano lesson. Their mothers also come, watch the class, take notes on new material and assignments and participate in some of the games. There is always a mini-recital at the end of the hour.

Although some little ones come once a week for a longer lesson, most of my preschoolers come twice a week for lessons. I schedule a small (3–6) group of children and their mothers (or dads) for approximately 1–1½ hours each session. The lessons include individual work at the keyboard with one child and parent while the others observe the lesson and wait their turn. I keep a few quiet toys and books in the studio to occupy active minds and hands while their ears listen to the lessons.

Since the Suzuki approach stresses early learning of the instrument without reading the music, I schedule theory only twice each month for the younger students. Replacing a regular lesson time, the class gives the children a chance to play the beginning theory games and perform a solo or two at the close of class.

The mothers tell me that their children always look forward to the theory classes. "Mary finds a great deal of pleasure in playing the piano, but you can't imagine how much she loves theory!"

To Illustrate

Recently, we had unusually beautiful weather after several weeks of cold, wet days. Before class the mothers and children had gathered outside, the mothers sharing practicing ideas and the children ages 3–6 scampering around the lawn in and out among the trees. By the time they came inside for class the children were full of energy. As I was ready to begin class they were still laughing, pushing and horsing around. No amount of prodding from their mothers could settle them down. Finally I spoke up.

"You all have a choice today." I told them as I reached for the stack of alphabet cards. "You can go back outside and play or settle down and play some theory games with me."

As the children looked at each other, I could sense their mothers thinking that this was a dangerous question to ask them.

After a moment, the children glanced around once more, smiled, and said, "Theory!"

What to Play When.

The chapters are numbered consecutively with the easier games in the beginning and the more advanced games toward the end. However, this doesn't imply that they should be presented in order from beginning to end. The games are grouped according to subject and many should be taught simultaneously. (see chart on page 12.)

Although this "time chart" is what I often follow in presenting the games, I suggest you use it only as a guide in developing your own program. The age of the students and their playing levels will determine what games can be played at the same time. Be adaptable.

How Long.

If you want to know how much time to spend on a game or how old the children should be when learning a particular game, I don't have the answers. All I can say is that speed isn't as important as learning the subject thoroughly. The pictures included in this book purposely show children who were introduced to music and to theory at different ages.

The objective in developing this approach was never to enable a child to learn note reading quickly, but to develop a good foundation for understanding the concepts of music theory. So gauge your presentation of the materials to the children with whom you're working. Move along at a steady pace and spend as much time as is needed on a particular area. But by all means, don't belabor a subject to the point of boredom. Keeping things lively will help stimulate interest.

Each teacher must develop that genius for finding the fine line between boring the students and pushing them too hard. Hopefully, the variety of games presented in this book will help along these lines.

ALPHABET CARDS	STAFF	RHYTHM	SIGNS	DICTATION	INSTRUMENT	SCALES
ABCDEFG	Intro TC	Blue jello	Dynamics	Dic. W/#	People on the piano	
↓	↓	↓	↓	↓	↓	
Snakes	Bingo	Blue jello too	Others	Dic. w/notes	Staff/piano	
↓	↓		↓	↓	↓	
Thirds	Teaching TC		Big pyramid	More notes		
↓	↓	↓	↓	↓		
	Teaching BC	Real rhythms	Tempos	Song puzzle		Major scales
↓	↓	↓	↓	↓		↓
Intervals	TC + BC	Other meters				
↓	↓	↓				
Major triads	Ledger lines					
→	→	→				

TC = Treble clef
BC = Bass clef

How Much in One Class?

We usually play a variety of games during each session selecting one or two from different areas. Some games may be played for only a few minutes, but the repetition for a short amount of time over several weeks is more beneficial than one longer time only once a month. The children's ability to retain the information will improve. If a new subject is introduced we may spend most of the time on that and play less of other games.

Here are samples from several levels of classes. The first could be a class of young preschoolers and the rest of older children.

Fix the order
Fat snake
Bingo
Blue jello
Some movement games

Variations on snake—thirds
Pick a pair—treble clef
Find the jellos
Follow that sign
Dictation with numbers

Dictation with notes
Staff card pairs
Real rhythms
I see . . .
Thirds scrabble

Song puzzle cards
Flat major scales
Playing sight-reading songs
Bingo both clefs
Write a song

Time is always set aside for each child to play a solo. This opportunity to perform each week allows the children to be quite comfortable when they play at recitals and other events. Although the mood is always informal and full of smiles, each child first announces the name of his piece and the composer and bows before and after his performance. The audience is generous with cheers, applause and good manners.

In those classes where the children are either beginning sight-reading or doing a steady diet of sight-reading, they're encouraged to follow along in the music book during each others' performances. This can also be great preparation for reading music. Once children have taken some melodic dictation and played games in Chapter 14, The Long and the Short, they'll begin to be able to follow the note and rhythm patterns as they hear the music.

Group or Private.

Perhaps your situation doesn't lend itself to forming theory classes or you'd prefer including theory during the private lesson. Feel free to do so. Although the majority of the games are described as group play, there are not many that can't be adapted to fit the private lesson situation.

And the opposite is also true. Some games show only one or two children in the photos or drawings. With simple improvising they can be played with more children.

On the Floor.

You'll notice as you glance at the photos in this book that the classes are always conducted on the floor rather than at desks. I find that children are most comfortable playing games on the floor. To me, that was the most logical place to be. It provides us with flexibility of movement and a feeling of intimacy.

Pacing a Game.

Through correspondence one year, I shared ideas about my games with a teacher in Switzerland who had heard of my teaching and wanted to use it with her students. That next summer she and her family took their vacation in the United States and she was able to come watch me teach at a Suzuki Institute in Ithaca, New York.

"Most fascinating," she told me after observing the first session, "I had no idea you move at such a fast clip while you teach. Not only does this take command of the children's attention so they won't miss anything, but helps to keep them from misbehaving."

Keep two thoughts ahead of the children, move quickly, speak clearly, and finish up a game before they begin to tire of it. It's fun!

The Magic of Non-Verbal Teaching.

Just recently I've begun playing certain games without the aid of speech. I explain to the children that we're going to try an experiment to see if we can read each other's minds. Instead of talking, I'll give them certain hand signals. Some of the signals I've adopted are:

Snapping my fingers once	They close their eyes
Two claps	They open their eyes
They raise their hands	They know the answer
I point to one child	He fixes the cards (or whatever)
Looking through rings made with my fingers	Leave your eyes open
Pointing to the parents and snapping my fingers	Parents close their eyes
Silent applause and smile	Correct answer

Many of the games are such fun to play non-verbally. If a note or card is turned face down and the student is to identify it, he can "write" the letter on the rug with his finger instead of saying it out loud.

With non-verbal teaching there is little need to discipline the children. Not only will they enjoy the excitement, but they have no choice but to watch you all the time so that they don't miss a signal. Their concentration will be easier without hearing your voice too.

Every Game?

As you look through this book you might wonder if it's necessary to play every single game. Without hesitation, the answer is *yes*, you can skip games. Not every child needs to play each game if they can still learn the concept and achieve success.

The results will be best if the games are played in sequence. Many games prepare the child for ones that will follow. If there's much skipping around, a child may have difficulty with a certain game because an earlier one was left out. Review old games for fun and reinforcement and to let the children see their progress. Occassionally, have a fun day when the children can choose their favorite games.

Names of Games.

The names of the games are mainly for the teacher's use. It's not necessary for the children to learn all the names although they do pick up many on their own by hearing the game referred to by name. Some classes give the games their own original titles.

Switching Roles.

You'll find that the children really love it if they can be the teacher some of the time. You can let a child mix up the alphabet cards while you close your eyes. They'll pay such close attention to see if you can make the cards right again.

Or let them write a rhythm for you to clap. Always pause thoughtfully before you act to give the game some suspense. Sometimes it's fun to not completely fix the cards or to leave out a blue or jello. How much fun for them to think they made the game so tricky that they fooled the teacher.

To Illustrate

One group of bright youngsters thought it was great fun to switch roles and take a card away while I closed my eyes. After several tries at tricking me, I heard excited whispers as I covered my eyes.

"Ready!" they shouted and laughed.

When I opened my eyes, they'd taken away every card. The rug was bare!

Reading Music vs. Music Theory.

The games in this book deal with prereading activities. However, this doesn't automatically insure that a child will be able to sight-read. Instead, the games should enable him to thoroughly learn the fundamentals of the notation of music. Because he's able to look at a page of music and understand what things mean and how they should be played, he can concentrate on the mechanics of reading.

The ability to sight-read is a skill that can be developed with a generous diet of just that—reading. It should be done regularly with a great amount of repetition on each level of advancement.

See that the child is looking at groups of notes with regard to their relationship to each other, up or down, repeated, and skips or steps.* Thinking of the letter names of the notes will slow the child down and not allow the music to flow. Help him to develop good eye-hand coordination habits from the beginning.

Encourage the child and he can be *terrific!*

*Mrs. Yurko is presently working on ideas to improve the techniques and skills of developing sight-reading abilities with her students.

3
Spinning
the Alphabet

Since the first seven letters of the alphabet are an integral part of note reading, it's logical to begin our study with them. Many youngsters can quickly rattle off the alphabet, but how thoroughly do they know the first seven of those letters?

Can they say them backwards? Can they tell you which letter comes before E without hesitating? Do they know if the letter that follows B looks like this 'C' or like this 'Ɔ'?

The games in this chapter will train the children to focus in on the seven letters: A, B, C, D, E, F, and G. The children will be delighted with the challenges presented them and begin forming a solid foundation for learning to read music.

GAMES FOUND IN THIS CHAPTER

GAME 1–A	:	*WHAT LETTER IS THIS?*
OBJECTIVE	:	To determine if the children can identify the letters: A, B, C, D, E, F, and G.
MATERIALS	:	Alphabet cards — two sets, two colors
PROCEDURE	:	With the children sitting before you on the floor, place the A card in front of them, smile and ask, "What letter is this?"

If their response is "A", then continue to find out if they can identify the remaining six letters *in sequence*. Stack the cards *on top of each other* so only one letter is showing at a time. This helps the child's attention by directing his eyes to focus on only one letter at a time.

If they identify the letters in the first set of cards easily, place the remaining set *out of sequence*, on top of the first set, one card at a time. Some children can say the letters in order but aren't as secure when they're out of order.

If the children identify some of the cards incorrectly, don't correct them, but continue through both sets of cards in order, letting them identify those they can. This game isn't designed for teaching letters and your corrections may only be confusing.

From this game you'll learn whether or not the children can identify the first seven letters of the alphabet. If they can, then you may go on to games like FAT SNAKE and others in this chapter.

GAME 1–B : *LEARNING LETTERS*

OBJECTIVE : A child may come to you unable to recognize all of the letters or be confused about the names of some of them. You can either teach him these letters or wait a few months and encourage his mother to play with letters at home. By waiting, he probably can learn the letters without your actually teaching him. In addition, he'll pick up a great deal by playing the games described after this one with children who know their letters. This game is a good one to play at home and also in lessons to help a child learn letters.

MATERIALS : Alphabet cards — two sets, two colors

PROCEDURE : In the first session concentrate on only the first one or two letters. Add more at the child's own pace.

Using one set of cards, place the letters in front of him, mixed up and not in a straight row. Take the A card from the other set of cards and tell him this is the letter A. Practice saying it together, then ask him if he can find the A in his cards.

"Good, Robert. You found it. Can you put it below to mine?"

21

After he puts it under yours, ask him to close his eyes. Rearrange his cards so the A is in a different place.

"OK, open your eyes and see if you can find your A and put it next to mine."

Repeat this, with many words of praise and many smiles until he can spot the A card easily. Say A aloud often. You can then try the same procedure with the B card.

After he seems to know which card is B, then you can play this game using A and B together, each time rearranging his letters. Remember to say the letters aloud often so he can get used to their names.

In the following sessions, review these letters and if they're secure, you can add others.

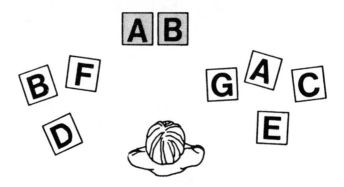

GAME 1—C : *FIX IT LIKE MINE*

OBJECTIVE : To help children learn the order of the letters.

MATERIALS : Alphabet cards — two sets, two colors

PROCEDURE : Line your cards up on the rug, in order facing the children. Hand out the second set and ask them to place the letters directly below yours, in order.

Explain that while their eyes are closed, you're going to switch around two of their cards. Switch two cards so they can see what you mean. The top row will remain in order for reference. Ask them to close their eyes. (NOTE: It's best not to say "don't peek". They really won't think to do so unless you suggest it. Instead you can say, "close your eyes really tight. Good.")

"OK, open your eyes. Can you find the ones I switched? If you can, raise your hand and after I call on you, you can fix the cards." Otherwise, everyone will dive for the cards. After one child fixes the cards, compliment him so he'll know that you're pleased. Say the cards together.

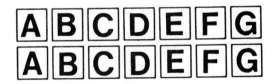

Chances are that they'll be able to spot the switches you make easily. Ask them to close their eyes and repeat until everyone has a turn.

Children delight in this game. It's easy, yet invaluable in helping them to learn the order of the alphabet. Even the shyest child will relax and begin smiling after you play this game a few times. Remember that they're being taught and not being tested. Help them to be right each time.

GAME 1–D   :   *FAT SNAKE*

OBJECTIVE   :   To have fun learning the order of letters.

MATERIALS   :   Alphabet cards – up to six sets.

PROCEDURE   :   Hand one set of cards to each child and keep one for yourself.

"Let's put all our A cards in a row." The children will look through their cards to find their A's. Help them to line up their cards next to each other.

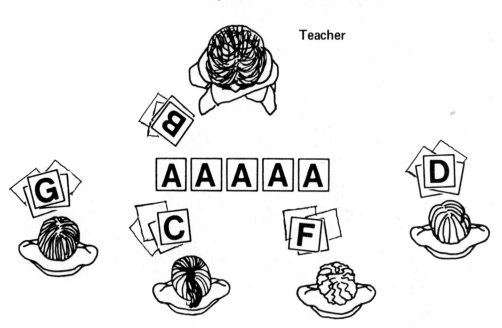

"Anyone know the letter after A? Right, it's B. Let's put our B's on top of our A cards." Help the children to match their colors.

As much as possible, let them put out the new letter before you do as you continue making the fat snake. Wait until all the cards of each letter are laid out before going on to the next letter.

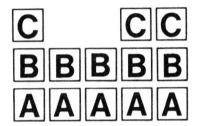

Remember not to correct them by turning their letters if they're upside down, sideways, or in the wrong column. Often they'll spot their own mistakes or another child will correct them. Continue on, one row of letters at a time until the fat snake is completed.

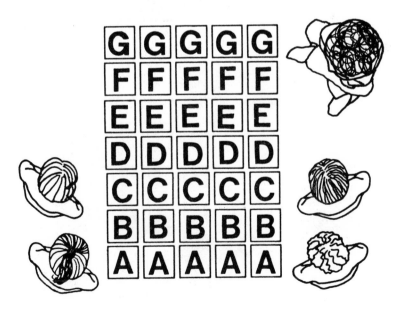

"Look at this fat snake we've made! You did a good job. Can we say the letters together? Let's go through one color at a time. Ready? A B C D E F G . . . A B C D E F G . . . A B C D E F G . . . A B C D E F G. Very good."

Saying the letters this way introduces the concept of saying A after G, a preview of the games to come.

Showing the children how to clean up the fat snake will establish the importance of always carefully cleaning up the games. Show the children how you can pick up only your color of cards, one at a time. Ask them to clean up their own cards and return them to you in order in a neat pile. (Very young children may find it too tricky to put the cards in order.) Thank the children as they return the cards to you.

It's enough to play this game only once in a session even if they ask for more. Then they'll look forward to doing it again.

You may wonder why the cards read up rather than down. The reasoning is since the letters read up on the staff, it's appropriate to place the cards going up as well.

VARIATION : In later sessions, you should sit back and let them make the fat snake by themselves.

Give each child one set of cards. After getting them started with the A and B cards, sit back and watch. As before, let them make and correct their own errors. If mistakes go unnoticed, they'll most likely be corrected when the children make the snake in later sessions.

VARIATION : A more sophisticated way to make a fat snake is to deal out all the colors so each child has several colors to play with. Let them make the snake as before.

26

GAME 1—E   :   *FIX THE ORDER*

OBJECTIVE   :   This game is like FIX IT LIKE MINE except it's played without the row of reference cards. It's always a favorite and the children never even suspect that they're practicing their letters.

MATERIALS   :   Alphabet cards — one set

PROCEDURE   :   Ask the children to lay out a set of alphabet cards in the correct order or do so yourself.

$$\boxed{A}\boxed{B}\boxed{C}\boxed{D}\boxed{E}\boxed{F}\boxed{G}$$

While their eyes are closed, switch two of the cards around.

A.M.

Ask them to open their eyes and raise their hands when they see the mistake. Call on one child to fix the cards.

$$\boxed{A}\boxed{B}\boxed{C}\boxed{D}\boxed{E}\boxed{F}\boxed{G}$$

After the cards are fixed, say them aloud together to check and to reinforce the order. Give everyone a turn.

Children delight in this game. The challenge of finding something that was mixed up while their eyes

27

were closed brings smiles of delight to any child's face. To encourage this and build confidence, begin with easy switches. Progress cautiously to more difficult switches only as the children are able to handle them easily.

One clever little boy enjoyed this game immensely. One day, he asked me why I thought he could find the switched cards so easily.

"Because you know your musical alphabet so well."

"No," he replied, grinning, "it's because I can hear which cards you move when they slide on the rug."

With that helpful bit of information, you may want to move the cards ever so quietly.

After playing this game and finding two cards easily, you may find the children enjoy the challenge of fixing three or more switched cards.

GAME 1–F : *WHAT'S MISSING?*

OBJECTIVE : This game is like FIX THE ORDER except you take away one card. It's a good one to play in the same session as FIX THE ORDER.

MATERIALS : Alphabet cards — one set

PROCEDURE : Lay a set of alphabet cards before the children in the correct order.

While their eyes are closed, remove a card. Leave the space open.

After the children open their eyes they can raise their hands when they've figured out which card is missing. After a child tells you, hand him the card and let him replace it.

$$\boxed{A}\boxed{B}\boxed{C}\boxed{D}\boxed{E}\boxed{F}\boxed{G}$$

VARIATION :   When the children are able, play the game as described above, except don't leave the space open. Push the remaining cards together to eliminate the space.

It's cute to notice how the children always check your hands to see if you've indeed removed a card.

GAME 1–G : *IS YOURS LIKE MINE?*

OBJECTIVE : To make FAT SNAKES a little more challenging, this game should be played only when you're certain that the children will be able to place the right cards in order. Remember that this game isn't designed to test the children, but to have more fun and suspense when making a FAT SNAKE.

MATERIALS : Alphabet cards — many sets

PROCEDURE : Give each child a set of alphabet cards and keep one for yourself. Line all the A cards next to each other on the rug.

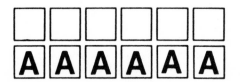

Placing your B card face down above the A card, ask the children what letter comes after A. They're to look through their cards and place their choices face down above their A cards.

"Let's see if they're the same." And everyone turns their cards to see if they're like yours. Continue placing cards face down and turning them over until you've used up all the letters.

30

GAME 1–H : *PICK A CARD*

OBJECTIVE : To allow the children to lay out the cards in order without any visual reference. This game helps you to see if the children have formed a mental picture of the order of the letters.

MATERIALS : Alphabet cards — one set for every two players

PROCEDURE : This game can be played with you and one child, you and several children, two children as a team, or a child and his parent as a team. Described is teacher and child playing as a team.

Hold a set of alphabet cards in front of a child as you'd hold a hand of playing cards. Let him pick a card and tell you what it is. Then he should place it on the rug between the two of you.

The child continues to pick one card at a time. After he names it, he should lay it down on the rug in sequence, leaving spaces for the cards still in your hand. Be certain the letters are reading left to right.

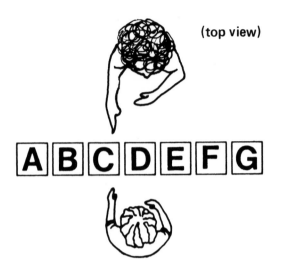

(top view)

If a mistake in order is made, let him finish all seven cards without any corrections from you. After all the cards are down, he may spot the error himself and correct it.

After all the cards are down *both of you should point to each card* in turn and say them together. Usually the child will see if he's reversed a letter or two and will quickly correct them. Help him if necessary. Then say them again to show that they're all correct.

It's then the child's turn to pick up the cards, mix them up and hold them for you to pick from. Pick one card at a time, identify the letter and place it on the floor, right side facing you. After you've picked all the cards, point to them together, saying them aloud.

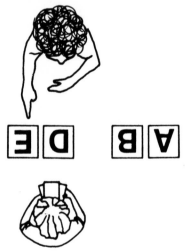

To Summarize the Steps

(Two children playing together.)

1. Linda holds the cards for Kathy who draws one card at a time, placing them on the rug in alphabetical order.

2. After all the cards are down, both girls point to each letter in turn, saying them out loud.

3. Kathy picks up the cards and holds them for Linda. She draws the cards one at a time and places them in order on the rug facing her.

4. Both girls point to the letters and say them aloud.

5. Linda picks up the cards and holds them for Kathy.

6. This continues for several turns.

4
Make
A Snake

Once the child has mastered the forwards order of the letters A–G, he's prepared to tackle more sophisticated games with the alphabet cards. Music doesn't always contain melodic or harmonic patterns within the bounds of A–G. We may have long scale passages beginning on any note, or intricate melodic material moving in and out of the pattern A–G. The games in this chapter prepare the child to think in these liberated terms.

GAMES FOUND IN THIS CHAPTER

A.M.

GAME 2–A   :   *SNAKE!*

OBJECTIVE   :   To teach that the music alphabet doesn't end with G, but begins again with A B C . . . The snake is a representation of the keyboard.

MATERIALS   :   Alphabet cards — many sets

PROCEDURE   :   Mix up two sets (two colors) of alphabet cards on the floor between you and the children.

        "Let's lay them out in order. A . . . B . . . C . . . Good. Next is . . . right, D. Let's keep going. Either color is fine."

Help them to place the A after G. "Did you know that there is a letter after G in music? We start over again with A." Let them finish the snake.

"Did we use up all the cards? Let's say them together. A B C D E F G A B C D E F G. Good. The music alphabet can go on and on just like a long snake. Let's add another color and make a longer snake of alphabet cards."

Push the two sets of alphabet cards together and toss in another color. Help them to begin their snake, but as they get the idea, move away and let them finish it alone.

"Good! You got all the cards out in order. Let's say them together." Point to the cards (or have a child point) in sequence to direct their attention.

Push the cards together in a pile, throw in another set of another color, and away they will go again. The kids will love making the snakes. You can continue until five or six colors are involved.

This game is self-correcting. If the children make an error in the letter order do not interfer and point out the mistake. They will find it themselves in order to finish the snake.

"Good snakes. OK, let's clean up. Nancy, can you get all the yellow? Craig, the green. Susan, the purple. Michael, the blue and Becky, the pink. Please stack the cards in order with A on the top and G on the bottom." Clean-up becomes another chance to practice the letters.

VARIATION : Divide the children into three small groups. Three groups are better than two so the game doesn't become a race and turn into a competition. Give each group three sets (three colors) of cards and get them started on a snake. Since this isn't a race, it doesn't matter when they begin.

The children will make their snakes quickly and

can be instructed to call out "SNAKE" when they're finished. Then you can rush over and admire their snake. Without warning, mess it up and toss down a fourth color of alphabet cards.

"That was great. Can you make even a *longer* snake?"

It isn't necessary to pass out the cards, just have them close together on the floor so whoever sees the right card can put it into the snake. It's also best not to request a specific color sequence unless the group decides on this. The main thing is the order of the cards and the colors just make it more fun.

Depending on how much room and time you have and the age of the children, you can continue this until all three teams have made snakes using five or more colors of alphabet cards each. End by having everyone read their snakes out loud in unison.

"OK, let's clean up. How fast can you get all the cards to me, separated by colors, in order and in neat piles?" Clean-up becomes as much fun as making the snakes.

VARIATION .   After a team has finished their final snake and you have admired their work, ask them to close their eyes. Mix up the letters.

"Guess what I'm doing . . ." You can laugh and tease them.

"You're mixing them up!"

"Right!"

Have them open up their eyes and correct the snake.

VARIATION :   After a snake is finished you could also turn 6 - 12 cards face down while the children close their eyes. After opening their eyes they can take turns identifying the letters for the others in the group.

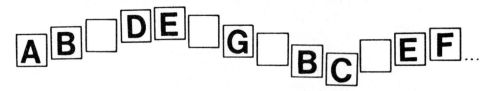

GAME 2—B   :   *VARIATIONS ON SNAKE!*

OBJECTIVE   :   To give the children practice beginning on any letter of the musical alphabet, even backwards.

MATERIALS   :   Alphabet cards — many sets

PROCEDURE   :   *START NOT WITH A.* Make snakes as described in the previous game except begin on a letter other than A. Be sure to say the snake through when finished.

     TAIL FIRST. Once it's easy for the children to make snakes, make them backwards, starting with the tail end first. This game will make more sense to the children if you first make a snake forwards then read it backwards.

     Place a G card to the right of the children. The next card F should be placed to the left of the G card. Let the children continue placing cards, making the snake backwards. The snake should read A B C D E F G A B . . . etc., from left to right when it's completed, so it's in the same order as a piano keyboard.

GAME 2—C   :   *FINE!*[1]

OBJECTIVE   :   To give the children individual practice laying out the alphabet cards in order quickly.

MATERIALS   :   Alphabet cards — one set for each child

PROCEDURE   :   Give each child a set of cards and ask them to spread out so each of them has enough room to lay out their cards. Ask each child to put his A card on the rug to his left and mix up the rest on the floor.

After you call out "GO", the children are to arrange cards in order A B C D E F G. When they finish, they are to call out "Fine". Some children will naturally be able to go faster than others. It's important for no one to feel that they're the slowest. They'll understand if you ask them:

"When we're playing music, is it better to play the notes as fast as we can or to play it so that all the notes and everything else is right? So when we play FINE!, what is more important—to finish first or to get your cards right?"

"To get your cards right."

"OK, let's try it. Leave your A cards out and mix up the rest. Keep mixing them with your hands until I call 'Go'." Call out "Go" and away they'll go.

It's easy for the children to play FINE!, starting with other letters. After they've completed a round of FINE!, take one child's A and place it at the end of his cards to read B C D E F G A.

"Now we have cards that begin with B and end with A. This is OK, isn't it?"

"Sure."

"OK, this time leave your B card out and mix up the rest." As they're quickly putting their cards out, remind them that B is to be the first card and A the last.

Introduce each new order of letters in this manner.

---

[1] Pronounced fē′nā, to finish, (the direction marking the close of a repetition of music).

If you should see someone's cards out of order, ask everyone to point to their cards and say them in order in unison. Anyone with an error will most likely fix it. If not, make a mental note to play this and other card games in class next week. This is more productive than singling out the child with the mistake in front of his peers. Or, without saying any verbal correction, casually rearrange his cards so they're correct.

GAME 2–D : *ARE THESE THREE RIGHT?*

OBJECTIVE : To teach children to isolate short segments of the alphabet since music often deals with short note patterns as well as long scale patterns.

MATERIALS : Alphabet cards — three sets, three colors

PROCEDURE : While the children's eyes are closed, lay out three cards from each set. The example will be A F B – G D C – B C D. Arrange the four remaining cards above the row of three cards.

Tell the children that the cards in the row may be either right or wrong. If the card is wrong, they're to exchange it with the correct one from above. The only rule is that the first card or each set of three must remain first in the row. They can take turns fixing the cards. The corrected cards would read:

Begin this game with easy patterns like the ones shown above. If a child experiences difficulty correcting a pattern, you can help by slowly saying the alphabet out loud. Easy patterns to correct are ACB, DEG, CED, EBG, while harder ones are AFE, EDG, GBA, and FCA.

GAME 2—E   .   *AFTER AND BEFORE*

OBJECTIVE   :   To develop recognition of the letters after and before a certain letter, relying on memory rather than visual reference.

MATERIALS   :   Alphabet cards — two sets, two colors

PROCEDURE   :   Place three consecutive letters of one color before the children while their eyes are closed. Keep the remaining letters in your hand. The second set of cards should be mixed up and placed below the three cards.

Ask the children, "What letter comes after D?" The child you call on will find the E and place it after the D.

"Very good! Now, which card comes before B?" Call on one child to place A to the left of B.

Ask the children to close their eyes. Return the cards and place a new set of cards before them. This can continue for several rounds, giving each child several turns.

When the children demonstrate skill with three cards, use only two cards. With less visual reference, they must rely more on their memories.

When they can do two cards easily, place just one out.

If you want to give them even more challenge, toss down just one card and ask what letter comes either before or after it. With no visual reference, the children must rely entirely on their memories. It's probably best if they respond as a group.

One group of four and five year olds made great sport of an opportunity to be the teacher. While I covered my eyes, I could hear whispers as they arranged the three cards. When I opened my eyes, I saw DEF in a neat row before me. But when I looked for C and G, I discovered they had hidden them from me!

GAME 2—F : *PHILL'S SCRABBLE*

OBJECTIVE : Developed by a friend, this is a great game which will give the children practice on their letters. It's self-correcting and loads of fun.

MATERIALS : Alphabet cards — many sets

PROCEDURE : Without using specific colors, lay out the beginnings of a scrabble game in the middle of the floor for the children.

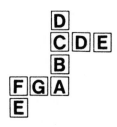

Once they've caught on to the idea, toss the re-maining cards to one side of the room. Instruct them to bring over *one card* at a time and add it correctly wherever they want. If they see a card in the wrong spot they're free to remove it. Letters are to read only across from left to right and from bottom to top (like the FAT SNAKE), however, they can be built on in any direction.

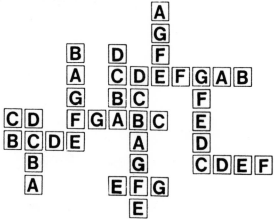

You should step away and let the children play this without your advice or help if mistakes do occur. After several sessions, they'll be able to do this without errors.

Clean-up can be just like in SNAKES.

45

GAME 2—G   :   *ALPHABET BEADS*

OBJECTIVE   :   To give the children practice with their musical alphabet.

MATERIALS   :   Alphabet beads — each bead has one letter on it

PROCEDURE   :   In my music studio I have a basket of beads and two knotted shoe strings out on a table. While the children are observing each others lessons and theory classes they are free to play with beads, stringing them in order just like the alphabet snakes.

As the children become more advanced with their theory lessons they can string the beads in thirds and other intervals.

They can also be used to practice the order of sharps used in major scales.

Or the order of flats.

Or the major scales using sharps.

Or the major scales using flats.

5
This Line
and That Space

As you "spin the alphabet" and "make snakes", you can introduce the concept of lines and spaces. The musical line and space are not what they're in school. Children are taught to write on the line, but actually they're writing in what in music is known as *the space*. Our line notes are right on the line. So don't be surprised at any initial confusion of this idea.

BOTH WRITING ON THE LINE

A common oversight of sight-readers is to jump into a piece on the first notes and sprint ahead, perhaps forgetting to check the position of the clefs, the key and the meter. Then suddenly, the ear hears something wrong and the eyes try to look back to the beginning of the piece to find out what to correct.

Help your students to become aware of this important information found at the beginning of each piece from early studies. Clef signs need not be taken for granted nor time and key signatures dismissed as too confusing. Instead, the student can learn to concentrate on what notes to play.

It's up to the teacher to develop good habits early. The child will be more aware of the clefs if they aren't permanently drawn on all the clefs. If the children are free to handle the clef and place it correctly on the staff, they'll be more conscience of them and the other important information they'll learn later.

GAMES FOUND IN THIS CHAPTER

GAME 3—A : *INTRODUCING TREBLE CLEF*

OBJECTIVE : To present the staff and the treble clef.

MATERIALS : 1) One-staff board
2) Treble clef

PROCEDURE : With the children sitting before you, place the one-staff board flat on the floor in front of them. Dangle the treble clef in front of them.

"This is a treble clef. I'll pass it around so you can all feel it." Let the children handle the clef, feeling its curves and shape.

After it's returned to you, tell them that this treble clef has another name, G clef. Practice saying the names together. Even young children can pick up the names easily if you say them out loud many times during this and other lessons.

To help the children see that the clef isn't just a random collection of shapes, they can practice tracing it with you. The arrows show the direction to take.

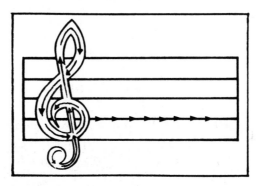

Little children can take turns following your finger around as you say:

"Start at the bottom, all the way to the top, over to the big side, around the circle, and out onto G. G. G . . ." The children will laugh as you say "G G G . . ." and move your finger across the "G line."

As the children get older, they should learn the correct placement for the G clef.

The curly part on the bottom of the clef faces this direction:

49

The bottom of the big circle sits right on the bottom line:

And there's a bit of space between the clef and the vertical line:

Point to these three details carefully with your finger. With older children, they might enjoy comparing with the music.

To let the children practice taking turns placing the clef, ask them to close their eyes while you move the clef to a funny position. They'll giggle when they open their eyes.

GAME 3–B : *NOTE TOSS I*

OBJECTIVE : To teach the difference between a line and a space.

MATERIALS :
1) One-staff board
2) Treble clef
3) Toss note
4) Plastic ledger line sheet
5) Pencil or stick

PROCEDURE : With the children sitting in a semi-circle on the floor, place the staff board between you and them. Let the children help you place the treble clef in the correct place. They may enjoy tracing it as in the previous game.

Take the toss note and place it on a line, saying *line*. Move the note to other lines saying the word line as you do.

Place the note on a space and say *space*. Do this with all the other spaces.

50

Then move the note randomly from lines to spaces, saying the words aloud. The children will join in and say the words with you as soon as they understand the concept.

Ledger lines are easy to introduce.

"We also have lines and spaces above and below the staff. The lines are called *ledger lines*." Place the plastic ledger line sheet on the staff and place the toss note on it. The children can call out line or space as you move the note. Include notes above and below the printed staff.

To play toss, place a stick or pencil a little more than one foot below the staff. The children can stand behind the stick and take turns tossing the note, calling out if it lands on a line or a space. If the note doesn't land right on the line or the space, you can move it a little.

A.M.

The students often enjoy choosing the next person to toss after they've taken a turn. I suggest to them that they choose the person who's being the quietest.

GAME 3—C : *INTRODUCING BASS CLEF*

OBJECTIVE : To introduce the bass clef and learn its placement on the staff.

MATERIALS : 1) Two-staff board
2) Clef signs

PROCEDURE : Once the children understand about lines and spaces and the treble clef, they can learn about the bass clef and how it's placed on the staff. They should also learn that the other name for the bass clef is the F clef.

Let them practice placing both the treble and bass clefs on the correct staves, making sure they understand which clef belongs where. While they have their eyes closed, move the two clefs so that they're in the wrong places on the staves. After the children open their eyes, they can take turns fixing the clefs.

NOTE: If you'd rather, you can introduce the bass clef on the one-staff board using just the bass clef.

The shape of this clef is easier to understand, but the children will enjoy it if you say "ffffffff" as you move your finger around the clef (start from the "ball") and say "dot-dot" for the 2 dots.

GAME 3—D : *NOTE TOSS II*

OBJECTIVE : To learn about the "invisible" middle line and to practice identifying the clefs.

MATERIALS : 1) Two-staff board
2) Clef signs
3) Toss note

PROCEDURE : Place the staff board on the floor and let the children place the clefs in their proper places. As review, move the toss note around on the staff letting them call out space or line. Talk about the fact that although there isn't a line drawn on the staff, there is an "invisible" line in the middle between the two clefs. It's just another ledger line. Drill them on this.

This game is played just like NOTE TOSS I. The children can take turns standing behind a pencil and tossing the note onto the staff. Not only should they call out line or space, but what the two names of the clef is that their note landed in. If it lands on middle C, they can name both clefs. Help them to say the correct clef.

Following a theory class demonstration one summer, an elderly woman came up to share some feelings.

"I have been teaching piano for over twenty-five years. There's one thing I feel strongly about. If not taught correctly, children somehow get the incorrect notion that there's a bass clef and a treble clef, and never shall the two meet. Somehow, they don't see how close the two really are. I think this particular game helps to teach this correctly." This is important and should be stressed to the students.

If you look at a grand staff of regular printed music, you will see quite a bit of space between the two clefs to allow for any ledger lines. However, on the two-staff board, there is room for only middle C. This should help the children to understand the relation of the two clefs easier.

GAME 3—E : *PRE-BINGO*

OBJECTIVE : To preview the concept of the bingo cards for young children.

MATERIALS :
1) One-staff board and clef sign
2) Bingo note (same as toss note)
3) Bingo cards
4) One bingo dot

PROCEDURE : Place the staff board in front of the children with the bingo cards in one pile near it. Explain that the bingo card has four small staffs just like the big staff board. Point out the different line and space notes drawn on the card. Place the bingo note on the staff board on a note that's found on the bingo card. Taking a bingo dot . . . "I'm going to move this to each note on the card. Stop me when you see the same note that's on the staff board."

Do this several times with different notes and different cards until you're convinced that the children understand how to relate the notes printed on the cards to the bingo note.

Don't be surprised at their initial confusion—it's quite normal. Some children continue to reverse letters even after much exposure. Understanding high and low notes on the staff is really quite a sophisticated concept.

A.M.

GAME 3—F   :   *MUSIC BINGO*

OBJECTIVE   :   To help the children learn to differentiate between high
                 and low lines and spaces on the staff.

MATERIALS   :   1)   One-staff board
                2)   Clef sign
                3)   Bingo note
                4)   Bingo dots
                5)   Bingo cards

PROCEDURE :   Seat the children on the floor so that they can see the
               staff board. Give each child a bingo card. Ask each child
               to identify the 4 notes on his card as a line or a space,
               then give him 4 bingo discs. Explain that once the game
               begins, the cards cannot be turned. Sharp little Lisa
               could bingo in a hurry if she kept turning her card!

               If young children are playing, arrange the children
               so that their cards are turned the same direction as the
               one-staff board. It's expecting too much of young

children to be able to understand this game if their card is turned sideways.

To begin, place the bingo note on a line or a space on the staff board. The children are to look for that same note on their bingo card. If they have it they can **place a bingo dot on the note. If they don't have it,** they can wait for another turn.

Continue placing notes on the board, one at a time, giving the children a chance to check their cards. Try to keep things even so that everyone has about the same number of notes covered. If you see a child who doesn't have as many notes covered, glance over his card and use one of his notes on the next turn. This keeps everyone happy.

The object of the game is to fill up the bingo card with four covered notes. When that happens, the child can call out "Bingo". But never end there. With enthusiasm, continue to place notes on the staff until everyone has filled up their cards and called out bingo.

If you previewed this game thoroughly, the children shouldn't have trouble matching the notes. However, don't be distressed or correct the child if a few notes are covered out of turn or overlooked all together. As this game is played during other classes, the children will improve.

By keeping a watchful eye on the cards as the game is progressing, you can "fix" the game so that several children finish at once.

"Isn't that neat! Everyone covered all the notes on their cards. How smart you are today."

NOTE: If you're playing this game with very young children it's advisable for the mothers to join their children on the floor. Throughout the game they can gently encourage the children to place the notes correctly.

NOTE: While the name of this game is Bingo—you may wish to have the children review some musical terms at the same time. Before each round begins, select a musical term and discuss its meaning. When the child fills up his bingo card, he's to call out the term instead of "bingo".

56

GAME 3—G :   *INTRODUCING THE TREBLE CLEF NOTES*

OBJECTIVE :   To introduce the names of the notes in the treble clef. This is an excellent game to play nonverbally. It's not advisable to do all the steps in one class. Divide it over several sessions, reviewing previous steps before going on to new ones.

MATERIALS :   1)   Alphabet cards — two sets, one color
2)   Notes With Letters
3)   Treble clef
4)   One staff board

PROCEDURE :   *STEP ONE:* Tell the children: "I am going to show you a new way to line up the alphabet cards. Watch me closely and then I will let you do it. First I lay out the G."

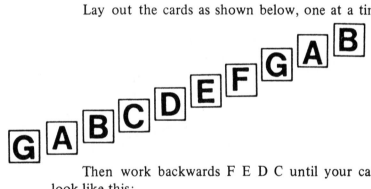

Lay out the cards as shown below, one at a time.

Then work backwards F E D C until your cards look like this:

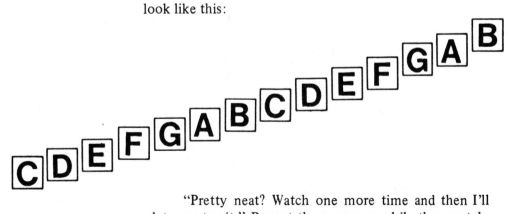

"Pretty neat? Watch one more time and then I'll let you try it." Repeat the sequence while they watch. "Ready to try it?" Deal out the cards to the children. Help them to put them out in the same pattern. G is first, then up in order to B, then backwards to C. If their mothers are present then . . . "Good! Let's give the cards to your mothers and see if they can do it as well. Mothers?" Repeat a few times.

STEP TWO: Take out the Notes With Letters, B C D E F G A B C D E F G A (one A and one C should be ledger line notes). Pass out the notes to the children. The alphabet cards should remain on the rug as shown in Step One.

"Watch me as I put these notes on in order on top of the alphabet cards." Put G on first, then up to B and then back to C. Leaving the alphabet cards on the rug, pass out the notes to the children. They should put on the notes in the same sequence you demonstrated.

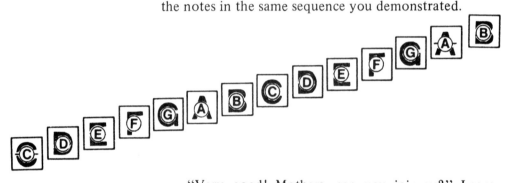

"Very good! Mothers, can you join us?" Leave the alphabet cards on the rug and pick up the notes with letters. Pass out the notes to mothers and children.

STEP THREE: Collecting the cards and the notes, you can say . . . "I bet if I took away the alphabet cards, you could still put out the notes in the right order. Want to try?"

"Sure. Let's try!" Pass out just the notes.

STEP FOUR: "Very good. That looked really easy. How about if I bring out the staff board and you line up the notes on it?"

Place the one-staff board in front of the children and let them place the treble clef on it.

Let everyone have a turn tracing the clef.

Tracing your finger over the G clef, explain that many hundreds of years ago this used to look like a letter G.[1] As you move your finger around the circular part of the clef, point out that this always circles the line G.

"The position of the treble clef tells us where the line G is. If I move the clef up like, this, where will the G be now?"

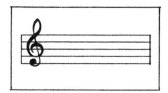

"Right, the third line." Move the clef around to other lines so they can relate the clef to the staff.

"In piano music, you will find the treble clef in this position. G will be on the second line.

"Watch me as I put the notes on the lines and spaces." Lay the notes on the staff beginning with G, just as you did with the cards on the rug.

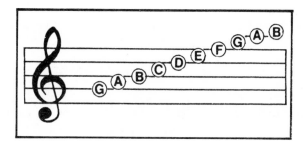

---

[1] Guido de Arezzo used the letters F and G as clefs in his Antiphonary, c. 1027. Gustave Reese, *Music in the Middle Ages*, (W. W. Norton & Company), p. 138.

Early forms of clefs are shown and discussed in the *Harvard Dictionary of Music* by Willi Apel, (Harvard University Press), p. 179.

The completed board.

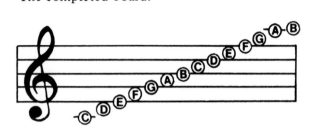

Pick up the notes and pass them out to the children and the mothers to place on the staff.

The children and mothers will like this game and find it easy to play. Ask the mothers to make a simple staff board, treble clef and notes at home for the children to play with. It can be easily made out of paper.

GAME 3—H   :   *INTRODUCING THE BASS CLEF NOTES*

OBJECTIVE   :   To introduce the names of the notes in the bass clef. This game will follow the same procedure used in the previous game INTRODUCING THE TREBLE CLEF NOTES.

MATERIALS   :   1)   Alphabet cards — two sets, one color
2)   Notes with letters
3)   One-staff board
4)   Bass clef

PROCEDURE .   *STEP ONE:* Place one F card out in front of them, facing the children.

Lay out the following cards in order as shown below.

Working backwards, lay out the cards down to D.

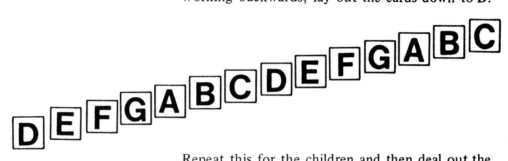

Repeat this for the children and then deal out the cards and let them try it. Deal out cards to children and mothers the second time.

STEP TWO: Take out the notes with letters, D E F G A B C D E F G A B C (one C and on E will be ledger line notes). Put the notes on the alphabet cards beginning with F, then up to C and then backwards down to D. You can repeat this, giving the children several turns and including the mothers if possible.

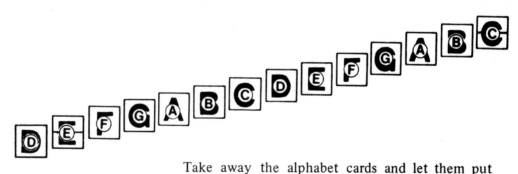

Take away the alphabet cards and let them put just the notes on the rug in the same sequence. This should be easy for them.

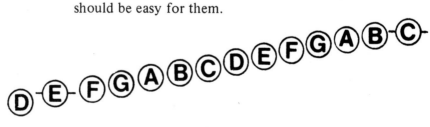

STEP THREE: Place the one-staff board in front of the children and let them place the bass clef on it. After they trace around the clef and "dot-dot" on the two dots, show them how to trace their finger out across the F line. As you did with the treble clef, explain how the position of the clef tells us where the note F is. Move the clef for them to find F in different spots.

Let them watch as you put the note on the staff beginning with F, up to A and then backwards to D. Deal out the notes to the children and let them practice it. This will be easy and fun for them.

6
Blue Jello

Which games are among the favorites? Surely, it's the rhythm games found in this chapter. Perhaps, it's because they don't require as much memory work as learning the names of the lines and spaces and there's the added dimension of sound and the fun of clapping.

Using the blue jello sticks simplifies the study of rhythm. After a few minutes even preschoolers can read the rhythms properly. Since there are no bar lines, there's no complication of dividing the measures to fit into a particular time signature.

Once the "two" rings are introduced, rhythms can even be in combinations of duple and triple time. It's a breeze to practice correcting rhythms and even take simple rhythmic dictation with the blue jello sticks. Rhythm understanding is essential. Try to incorporate it into every theory class.

GAMES FOUND IN THIS CHAPTER

A.M.

GAME 4—A   :   *BLUE JELL-O*

OBJECTIVE   :   To teach children to read simple divisions of the beat. The number of steps you cover in one session will depend on the age of the children.

MATERIALS   :   1)   Blue jello sticks
2) $\frac{4}{4}$ rhythm board - use face down

PROCEDURE   :   *STEP ONE:* Place the rhythm board face down in front of the children. Place about six of the longer sticks across the board in a row, spaced evenly about two inches apart. Although these sticks are meant to represent quarter notes, you can call them blues in these early stages of learning about rhythm.

"What color are these sticks?" you can ask.
"Blue," they answer.
"Right. Blue . . . Blue . . . Blue . . . " Point to the sticks as you say them and the children will join in saying the words with you. Pointing will help their eyes get accustomed to reading from left to right.
"Very good. Isn't this simple?"

64

STEP TWO: Show the children the shorter stick, comparing its length to the blue sticks.

"I have a shorter stick. When I place it across the top of two blue sticks, we can call this jell-o."

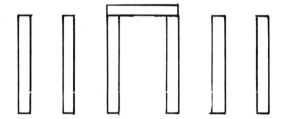

"Now this would read — Blue . . . Blue . . . Jell-o . . . Blue . . . Blue." The children will join you as you say and point to the sticks. Since the jello represents a pair of eighth notes, it's important to say them evenly, without any accent. Say jell´-o´. The children will imitate you, so be certain to say it correctly.

"I can move the jello stick another place. Let's try this one together."

Direct the children to begin together. Ready . . . Go can represent the up beat and then point to the first stick to begin.

You can continue adding more blues and jellos to make the rhythm longer. Even preschoolers are able to say these rhythms after a few minutes if you're careful to introduce the material in small steps. With the pulse at a medium tempo, the children should be able to say each new rhythm pattern after one, or at the most, two tries. Give the children lots of praise as they say the rhythms correctly.

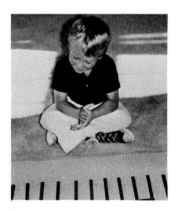

STEP THREE: Now comes your chance to build their confidence.

"OK, here's a new rhythm for you. I think it's pretty tricky. What do you think?" you say with a straight face.

"No, looks easy. That will be a cinch."

"OK, here goes. Ready. Go. Blue . . . Jello . . . My that was good. Here's another. Looks pretty hard to me."

"Never. This one's even easier."

"OK. Ready. Go. Jello . . . Blue . . . "

Soon the children will be saying how easy blue jello is and how you can't trick them. It's fun because even though you're saying they're tricky, each rhythm is as easy as the last.

STEP FOUR: After they've grasped the concept of blue and jello in relation to the sticks, you can introduce clapping of the rhythms.

"If I clap this," and clap once, "would it be a blue or a jello?" you ask.

"Easy. Blue."

"And this would be," clap two times, twice as fast.

"Jell-o."

"Great, let's clap these rhythms while we say them."

Clap with them in the beginning stages and encourage practice at home.

NOTE: Since I'm often asked the reasons for choosing the words Blue and Jello, I'll take a moment to explain. I wanted to use words with the right number of syllables for the particular notes—e.g. I could never understand the value of saying "half-note—half-note" for ♩ ♩ since the beat being spoken is really ♩♩♩♩ .

Having been intrigued with Dr. Seuss semantics, I began using colors blue and yellow for quarter and eighth pairs respectively.

After realizing that the word yellow didn't have a strong enough beginning we switched to jell-o and the the words stuck. As you will see in Chapter 14:The Long and The Short, the words are a great aid in helping the students to interpret visually the rhythms they've become used to hearing.

Another common question is what words I use for dotted quarter-notes, single eighth-notes or patterns in $\frac{6}{8}$ of $\frac{3}{8}$ meters. Presently, I'm not using words for all of these. When the "blue jello" words aren't always needed and the students can read and clap rhythms, they can usually imitate my clapping without the need for words. Feel free to do your own thing.

♩. = "blue" . . . (whisper) "jell" . . "o"   ♫♪ = "berrygoose"

♪♫ = "gooseberry"   ♪ = either "jell" or "o" when helpful

GAME 4—B : *CLAP BACK*

OBJECTIVE : To introduce the children to simple rhythmic dictation.

MATERIALS : 1) Blue jello sticks
2) $\frac{4}{4}$ rhythm board — use face down

PROCEDURE : Play this game after the children are comfortable clapping blue jello rhythms.

"I am going to clap something for you and I want you to tell me the words. Try this."

Clap ♩ ♫ by yourself.

"Blue jello," they should tell you.

"Good." Clap ♫ ♫ by yourself.

"Jello . . . Jello." Continue clapping short patterns for them to identify. Some combinations:

After the children get the idea of this dictation, let them take turns writing out what you clapped with the blue jello sticks. In the beginning use 4 - 6 blue sticks and one jello. Add more as they're able.

GAME 4—C : *FIND THE JELLOS*

OBJECTIVE : To give the children practice relating rhythms they hear, to how they should be written.

MATERIALS : 1) Blue jello sticks — only a few when first playing this game.
2) $\frac{4}{4}$ rhythm board — use face down

PROCEDURE : Line up the blues on the board, spaced evenly.
"I'm going to clap a rhythm for you to write." Request that they listen to the entire rhythm before placing any of the small sticks on the board.

Clap the rhythm evenly at a moderate tempo. Until the children become skilled at this game, say blue and jello as you clap. Later, just clap, letting them pick up the rhythm without verbal reinforcement.

After the child who wrote the rhythm indicates that he's finished, clap and say what he wrote. If the rhythm was written correctly, the other children will say so. If it isn't, most likely the child who wrote it has already corrected it.

GAME 4—D	:	*FIX THE JELLOS*
OBJECTIVE	:	To practice rhythmic dictation.
MATERIALS	:	1) Blue jello sticks
		2) $\frac{4}{4}$ rhythm board — use face down
PROCEDURE	:	Write out a blue jello rhythm pattern.

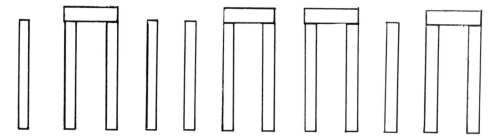

"I'm going to clap this for you, but I just might change something. Listen to the whole rhythm, then I'll let one of you move the jello stick."

Always have everyone clap the rhythm the child wrote, so they can compare to see if it's right. Be certain to move in small steps so the children can get them right.

As they become good at this, you can clap a rhythm with more than one error.

A.M.

69

GAME 4–E : *MOTHER, CLAP IT*

OBJECTIVE : To involve the parents in the blue jello game.

MATERIALS : 1) Blue jello sticks
2) $\frac{4}{4}$ rhythm board – use face down

PROCEDURE : Line up the blue sticks on the board. Hand a parent the jello sticks and let them write a rhythm for the children.

Or better yet, let each child write a rhythm for his or her parent. (Tip them off before class to take several tries before clapping it correctly.) The child will carefully arrange the sticks while the parent closes her eyes. Two hand claps, she leaves out a blue. "No!!" laughs her child, "you missed a blue!" All the children will watch so carefully and learn much more catching mothers make mistakes. Laughter and learning make a great combination.

A.M.

GAME 4–F : *BLUE JELLO TOO-OO*

OBJECTIVE : To introduce the half note value.

MATERIALS : 1) Blue jello sticks
2) Too rings
3) $\frac{4}{4}$ rhythm board – use face down

PROCEDURE :   For fun and to nonverbally emphasize that the too ring has a hole in it (and that the half-note is not colored in) challenge the children this way. Slip one ring on your finger.

"Do you think you can pass this ring clear around the circle going from finger to finger? Let's try!"

Slide the ring from your finger onto a child's finger sitting next to you who will pass it on around the circle. If you have a large group (over 10), pass another ring around the circle the other direction at the same time to see if both can come completely around and back to you. This is great fun.

Place a too ring on a blue stick explaining that we call this a "too". Emphasize that the too ring changes the blue into a too.

In order to feel the half note pulse, clap it like this: clap as you say "too-oo", letting your hands rise up, nearly to eye level, then return down on the second beat keeping your hands together. You can emphasize the second beat a little with your voice. Practice this with the children carefully.

As they are first learning toos, write rhythms with toos in pairs. Later, you can write combinations of duple and triple meters all in the same rhythm pattern.

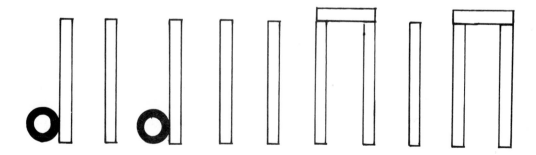

71

GAME 4–G   :   *MISSING BLUE–JELLO–TOO*

OBJECTIVE   :   The children will enjoy playing any of the games mentioned previously using the too rings in the rhythm patterns. Here's another.

MATERIALS   :   1)   Blue jello sticks
                            2)   Too rings
                            3) $\frac{4}{4}$ rhythm board — use face down

PROCEDURE   :   Write out a rhythm with the sticks and rings.
                            "I'm going to clap this rhythm, except I just might leave something out. Listen to the whole rhythm and then if you know what I left out, raise your hand." Clap the rhythm evenly, leaving out one thing. At this point, they should be able to do this without hearing the words.
                            When they can discover one thing that was left out, try leaving out two. Between turns, write a new rhythm.
                            Always keep a lighthearted mood and watch for smiles.

GAME 4–H   :   *BLUE PINEAPPLE JELLO WITH THREES AND FOURS*

OBJECTIVE   :   To introduce triplets (pineapples), whole-notes (fours), and dotted half-notes (threes).

MATERIALS   :   1)   Blue jello sticks
                            2)   A dot from an F clef
                            3) $\frac{4}{4}$ rhythm board — use face down

PROCEDURE   :   Once you introduce the too ring and let the children write some of their own rhythm patterns, they'll probably begin experimenting and laughingly ask you what a ring by itself or three sticks under a jello stick would be. These can be a lot of fun to learn, and just as easy as the others.

TRIPLETS: With a twinkle in your eye, ask if anyone would like to learn about pineapples today. Let them practice clapping and saying "pineapple" several times. Also let them practice saying "pineapple jell-o pineapple jell-o pineapple jell-o" so they feel the pulses correctly. Write out a pattern like the one shown here:

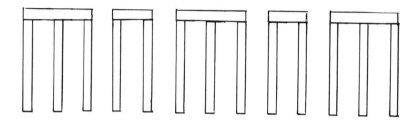

(Note: Use a blue stick across the top of three blues for the pineapple)

Practice clapping patterns using blues, jellos and pineapples. They'll enjoy this.

DOTTED HALF- AND WHOLE-NOTES: When someone asks about using a "too ring" by itself you can say, "Sure, that's fine by itself. We call it a for-or-or-or," and clap like you did for toos, adding two more pulses. Move your hands up and down as you say "or-or-or." They will catch on quickly.

Since we've used toos and fours, they may ask about threes. It's simple to add a dot after a too and say "three-ee-ee" and move your hands with your voice. Patterns like this one are a lot of fun.

GAME 4—I   :   *SONG FISH*

OBJECTIVE   :   This game, made up by Sheila Barnett of Geneva, Switzerland who is using my theory ideas with a group of Suzuki violin students, is so enjoyed by the students that I'd like to include it. It's objective is to introduce the concept of isolating the rhythm from a piece of music the children are very familiar with.

MATERIALS :   1)   Song fish — each fish has a picture representing one song
                2)   Fishing pole

PROCEDURE :   Select a number of fish which the children know or can play on their instrument. Let the children see the pictures on the fish so they know which fish represent which song. Spread the fish out on the rug in the middle of the children with the pictures face down.

Hand one child the fishing pole and let him pick a fish. (The fishing pole has a magnet on the end of the line which attracts the paper clip on the fish.) Being careful not to let any one see his fish, he looks at it and decides what song he's got.

After putting the fish down, he claps out the rhythm of the song he's drawn for the other children to guess. Ask the children to wait until the child is finished before calling out their answers.

Let all the children have a turn.

7
Thirds
and Triads

Once a student thoroughly knows the letters in the regular alphabet, A B C D E F G, it's time to introduce thirds. This should be done early in his musical studies since much of our music is based on Teritan harmony (chords built by thirds as opposed to other intervals). Thirds are easy to learn since they're just another way to spin the alphabet. Remember our early crutches?

> Every Good Boy Does Fine
> All Cows Eat Grass
> All Cars Eat Gas
> FACE
> Good Boys Don't Fight and Argue
> Great Big Dogs Fight Animals
> Empty Garbage Before Dad Flips

Our teachers were trying to teach us thirds. They just forgot to tell us what we're really learning and had us memorize those jingles instead. Without those crutches, what musical invalids we were. More important, many failed to teach us the incredibly simple fact that when you move from line to line, you are skipping a letter in the alphabet or a key on the piano. Why not tell children about thirds in the first place?

When you teach thirds first, then teach the names of the notes, you're progressing in two fun steps instead of one confusing step.

Step one: what thirds are.
Step two: their placement on the staff.

The concept of thirds should be thoroughly learned before attempting the names of the lines and spaces.

Thirds have another advantage. Later, when the students are learning to spell various kinds of triads and seventh chords, all they need to do is to concentrate on using the correct accidental, since spelling thirds is simple. And analyzing music isn't nearly as complicated, since the note letters need merely to be reshuffled to spell thirds.

GAMES FOUND IN THIS CHAPTER

GAME 5—A : *LEARNING THIRDS*

OBJECTIVE : To teach the concept of thirds.

MATERIALS : Alphabet cards — one set (later—more sets)

PROCEDURE : *STEP ONE:* By now the familiar alphabet cards are like old friends and have happy associations. Lay out one set of alphabet cards, A B C D E F G. As always, keep verbal explanations brief and to the point.

Point to the A card:

"This is the first card." Point to the B. "And this is the second card." Point to the C. "And this is the third card."

"If we move from the first card to the third card," pointing to the A and C as you speak, "we call this a third. The third above A is C." Give them a moment to absorb this.

"The third above C is E. The third above E is G." Continue with the other cards and the children will join in with the answers once they understand the concept.

"I wonder how smart you are today. Does anyone have an idea what the third above F is?"

"It's A!" They should answer easily.

"Right! You've got it! Now a really tricky one—how about the third above G?" They will study the cards.

"Is it B?"

"It sure is!"

Go over these thirds as a group, forwards and backwards.

STEP TWO: Tell the children that we're going to make a row of thirds out of a row of regular alphabet cards.

Slide the A card down beneath the row of cards.

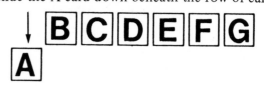

Pull down the C next, then E and G.

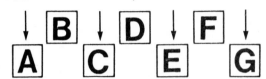

D and F can be moved out to the end one card at a time so that all the cards are in thirds. Say the letters out loud as you move them. Demonstrate this several times. Only one set of cards is used so the students can see that thirds, A C E G B D F is only a different arrangement of the regular alphabet, A B C D E F G.

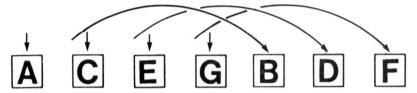

"Would anyone like to try this?" Hands will shoot up as everyone is anxious to try. Let them take turns on these cards so you can see if they understand the concept.

STEP THREE: Give each child a set of alphabet cards and let them practice putting cards in thirds, then back to regular alphabet, back and forth.

STEP FOUR: Lay out two sets of alphabet cards in alternating colors. One set will be turned face up, the other, in order, face down.

Point to one card at a time asking the children what the card is. After they respond correctly, turn the card over so they can see that their answer was right. This step reinforces the concept that thirds are just every other letter.

A.M.

GAME 5–B : *TOSS DOWN*

OBJECTIVE : To help the children memorize thirds. This game should move at a *very fast* pace.

MATERIALS : Alphabet cards — one set

PROCEDURE : Prepare the alphabet cards by putting them in thirds with A on top in a stack in your hand. Hold the cards facing you throughout the game so the children can't see them. Explain that as you toss down each card you want them to say them out loud with you.

Toss down the A card (facing the children) and say "A" as it hits the rug. "Good."

Place the card back in your hand. This time, toss down A and then C, saying the letters out loud. "A . . . C . . . Good!"

79

Return A and C to your hand and repeat. "A . . .
C . . . Good!" Place the E card face down next to the
C card. "Anyone have an idea what's under here?"

"I know," they should answer. "E."
"Right!" And turn the card over for them to
see.

Now, you have three cards to toss down.
"A . . . C . . . E." Everyone says these together
at a quick, even tempo. Continue adding one card
at a time as the children are able to say them with
confidence. You may want to do this over several
class sessions, sometimes playing with all the cards,
sometimes with just a portion of the cards. It's important to practice G B D F A extra.

To keep things interesting, toss the cards face
down a few times as everyone continues to say them
together. Do this without any warning.

Point to one card at a time, asking the children to
tell you the name of that card. If you go in order, this
should be easy. As they get more confident, point to
the cards out of turn, but always so they can answer
correctly.

VARIATION: Play TOSS DOWN a few times with
all seven cards in order, A C E G B D F. Without warning, toss the cards face down as described above. After
the children tell you the names of the cards, in order,
turn them back face down. Leave one card face up.

Checking to see that the children are watching,
move the A so it's the last card instead of the first.

Then point to the cards, out of order, asking the children to tell you the name of the card. Turn them face up as they answer.

Turn the cards face down again, leaving a different card face up. Move several cards from one end to the other. As before, let the children tell you which card is which. They'll find this a challenging game and pay close attention, if you move in small steps that they can answer correctly. As they become good at this, you may not need to leave one card face up.

To memorize the thirds and have a good time doing it, the children will enjoy playing some of the games found in previous chapters, SPINNING THE ALPHABET and LET'S MAKE A SNAKE. Play the games as described using thirds instead of the regular alphabet. Perhaps, you can make up a few of your own. One new game, 5—F: WHEELS is included before SNAKE!

GAME 5—C : *FAT SNAKE (THIRDS)*

GAME 5—D : *FIX THE ORDER (THIRDS)*

GAME 5—E : *WHAT'S MISSING? (THIRDS)*

GAME 5—F : *WHEELS*

OBJECTIVE : To give each student a chance to practice thirds with their own set of cards. The children often request this game, perhaps, because it's quite easy to play.

MATERIALS : Alphabet cards — one set per student

PROCEDURE : Give each player a set of alphabet cards and ask them to line them up in thirds—A C E G B D F.

After you say GO, the children are to take the A card and place it to the right of F, then take C and place it to the right of A, saying the letters as they move them. They are to continue taking letters from the beginning of their cards and placing them at the

82

end, moving in a circle around their body, moving as they do so, and thus forming "wheels". They can continue to go around and around until you call stop.

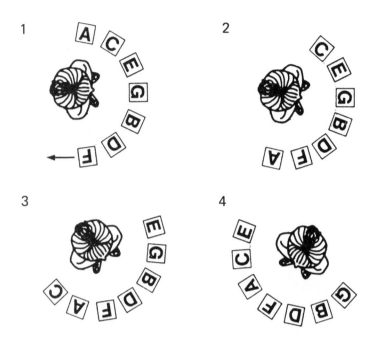

GAME 5—G : SNAKE!

A.M.

GAME 5—H : *VARIATIONS ON SNAKE (THIRDS)*

PROCEDURE : Start with one card in the center. Build in both directions, one card at a time.

OTHER VARIATIONS: Tail first—begin with F and build backwards.

Put an A and a F on opposite sides of the rug. Build towards the middle, one card at a time, keeping the ends even.

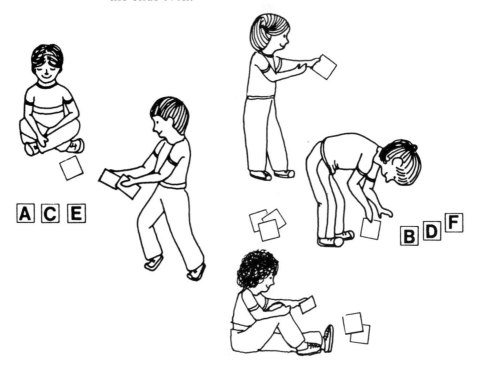

GAME 5—I   :   *FINE (THIRDS)*

GAME 5—J   :   *PICK A CARD (THIRDS)*

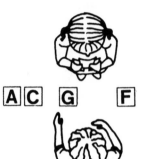

**top view
2 players**

A C   G   F

GAME 5—K   :   *AFTER AND BEFORE (THIRDS)*

G B D
F B A E C

GAME 5—L   :   *ARE THESE TRIADS RIGHT?*

OBJECTIVE   :   To introduce triads and prepare for the next game
                 WIN A TRIAD.

MATERIALS   :   Alphabet cards — three sets, three colors

PROCEDURE   :   Since triads are such an integral part of our music, you
                 can introduce the concept early. To give a familiar

86

association for the new word, you can discuss other words that also begin with "tri", such as *tri*cycle, *tri*angle, *tri*pods, and *tri*ceratops. Thus triads are three notes, or in this game cards, spelled in thirds.

Let the children practice dividing a row of third cards into threes. They'll be able to make several different triads. Since they already know thirds, the transition of placing the cards in triads shouldn't be difficult.

This game, ARE THESE TRIADS RIGHT? is played just like the game ARE THESE THREE RIGHT? except thirds are substituted for the regular alphabet letters.

Sample Problem

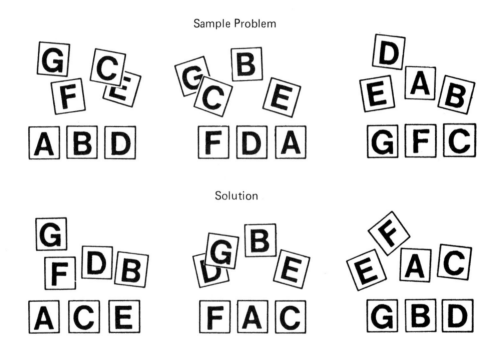

Solution

GAME 5–M   :   *WIN A TRIAD I*

OBJECTIVE   :   To have fun practicing thirds and triads.

MATERIALS   :   Alphabet cards — three sets, three colors

PROCEDURE : Deal out all the cards so each player has several cards. Everyone might not have the same number of cards.

The players are to hold their cards as if they were playing a "real card game" and should try not to let you see their cards. Very young children may need to spread their cards on the rug in order to see their cards.

Place one card in the center of the players. This card will be the root of the triad with the object of the game to build on the third and the fifth.

You can be the caller or if a younger sibling is present, he or she might enjoy taking part as the caller.

Let's say the root was a yellow A. The caller has called out green. Whoever has the green C should place it next to the yellow A.

Orange is called next. The player holding the orange E places it next to the green C. ACE is on the rug.

Because he put down the fifth, the green E, that player picks up the A and C cards and puts them in his hand with his other cards, ready for another play. The green E remains on the rug and slides over to become the new root for the next round.

And so the game progresses, often at a fast pace, as root, third and fifth are tossed down and then grabbed up. If one child should use up all his cards, collect a few from the other players so he can stay in the game. When time is up, the teacher calls out "last round" and the last hand is played. Whoever puts down the fifth in the last round picks up all three cards.

There is no need to call attention to the child who collected the most cards. Compliment *all* the children on how well they know their thirds and triads.

Since everyone has a mixture of cards, it might be fun to close this game by making a FAT SNAKE in thirds. It also makes clean-up easy. You'll find that the children love these two games and no one ever suspects that they're really practicing thirds!

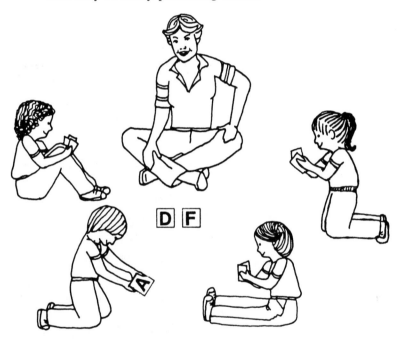

GAME 5–N   :   *WIN A TRIAD II*

OBJECTIVE   :   To practice thirds and triads. This game is just like WIN A TRIAD I except you play with two sets of each color so there are two of each card. This creates the added challenge of getting the right card down first. This game is excellent for older children and larger groups.

MATERIALS :   Alphabet cards — six sets, three colors (for example, two sets of green, two sets of yellow, and two sets of blue)

PROCEDURE :   Deal out all the cards and place one in the center of the children. Let's say it's a green F.

Yellow is called. Two players find that they have a yellow A. The first one to get his card down next to the green F can leave it there.

Then the players look through their hands for C's of any color in case their card is called. Blue is called.

The blue C is quickly placed next to the A and that player picks up the F and the A and places them in his hand. The other player with a blue C simply keeps it in his hand and gains no cards. The blue C becomes the new root.

I have found children to be exceptionally bright. However, it often takes a child a little time to look through all of his cards. You can help by not calling out the colors too quickly. Give the players a chance to look through their cards for the right third. Then call out a color and the right card will be tossed down quickly.

Since this game moves at a fast pace and can get quite exciting, some players may begin tossing down any card in hopes of having it right. To prevent this, tell them that any wrong cards simply come to you and are then out of play. This keeps everyone on their toes and mistakes less frequent. If someone runs out of cards, you can give him this pile or borrow some from other players.

Parents really enjoy being invited to join in this

game, although you may need to ask them to be careful not to become so involved that they play too fast for the children!

VARIATION: Use four cards instead of three and play for 7th chords. Or five cards and play for 9th chords.

GAME 5–O	:	*THIRDS SCRABBLE*
OBJECTIVE	:	To practice thirds, triads and seventh chords.
MATERIALS	:	Alphabet cards — many sets
PROCEDURE	:	This game can be played just like PHILL'S SCRABBLE which is found in a previous chapter, except the order of cards should be thirds and not regular alphabet.

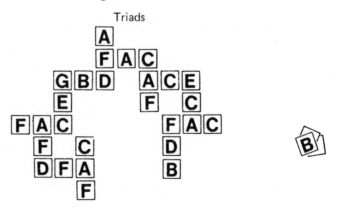

Scrabble

As the children become more comfortable with thirds and triads, you can ask them to only build triads. Such a scrabble game could look like this.

Triads

You can introduce the concept of seventh chords as just a triad with one more third and ask for only seventh chords in the scrabble game.

Seventh Chords

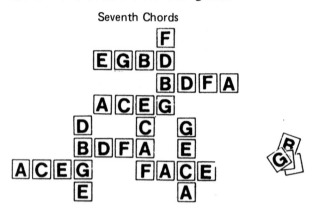

Later, when the children's theory studies advance, they can put in the proper accidentals.

Major Triads

GAME 5—P : *SHOW ME*

OBJECTIVE : To let the children see that they really are learning their thirds. Play this game only when you're certain everyone knows their thirds.

MATERIALS : Alphabet cards — one set for you and one for each child

PROCEDURE : Give each child a set of alphabet cards and keep one for yourself. Select one of your cards and place it face up in front of the children. Let's say it's the letter G.

The children are to look through their cards for B, the third above G. They're to take that card out and place it face down on the rug in front of them. When all the children have placed a card on the rug, call out "show me". They can turn their cards over to see if their answer is right. You can also place your B face down next to the G and turn your card up after saying "show me".

Continue placing a different card on the rug.
SHOW ME can also be played by asking the children to find the third *before* the card you put down. When they become skilled at this, you can ask them to place two cards face down, the third before and the third after.

GAME 5—Q : *INTERVAL CIRCLE*

OBJECTIVE : To teach the concept of intervals.

MATERIALS : STEP ONE   Alphabet cards — two sets same color

STEP TWO   Alphabet cards — one set for each student

PROCEDURE : *STEP ONE:*

Lay out two sets of alphabet cards in a row.

A B C D E F G A B C D E F G

"The interval from A to C is a third, right? Then A to D is a fourth." Talk about the other intervals and help the children learn the names.

After they grasp the concept, practice starting on different letters.

Call out a letter. "C . . . What would be the fifth above?"

"G."

"Right! Try E. A third above."

"G."

"Right! Try D. An octave above." And so on. Also do intervals below the letter you call out.

STEP TWO: Ask the children to join hands and make a circle. Then they should drop hands, turn around so they're facing out. Ask them to sit down.

Give each child a set of alphabet cards and ask them to make a big circle with the cards, with the children on the inside. They should start their letters with A, spelling the regular alphabet and have their first and last cards close to the person's cards next to them. It's helpful not to place two children with the same color of cards next to each other.

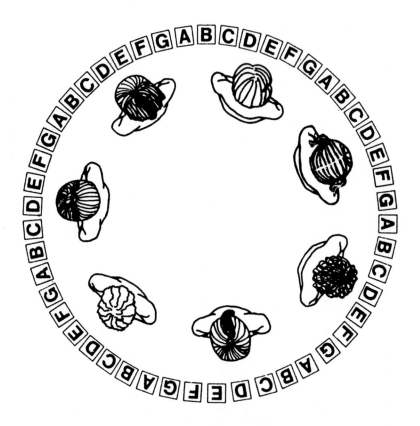

If the children have trouble getting their circle even, ask them to step away from it. They will then see how to fix it. After they are sitting back inside the circle, facing out, explain:

"I'm going to call out a letter . . . A. Everyone put their hand over and not touching an A card. Good. Move you to slap it and call out the letter . . . GO!"

After the game gets going, all you need to say is "B . . . Octave above . . . GO." or "C . . . Fifth below . . . GO." Always allow time for everyone to find the right interval.

Now for the fun. If someone slaps before you say GO, they must step out of the circle and wait a turn or two before going back in. It's kind of like "simon says," but always in a light-hearted mood.

VARIATION: See Chapter 12, Play it Again—Dictation Game 10—L — INTERVAL CIRCLE DICTATION

A.M.

96

8
Lines
or Spaces

Once they thoroughly know thirds, the children may begin memorizing the names of the notes on the staff. As they learn to identify these notes, you may want to wait on relating them to specific sounds or patterns on the piano. Instead, let the children's knowledge of thirds aid them in learning the staff.

There's no value in teaching jingles to learn the lines and spaces. It's more meaningful for the child to understand the concept of thirds behind the lines and spaces. When adults say a jingle like "every good . . . ", the spelling comes to mind and simultaneously "every" is associated with the letter E. Young children, on the other hand, don't think of the letter E when saying "every", so the jingle is useless.

An older child, seeing the fourth line on the treble clef loses valuable time if he must point to each line in turn saying the jingle. He should know the notes instantly.

The games in this chapter deal only with practicing lines *or* spaces of one clef. Following are the suggested steps for memorizing the names of the lines and spaces on the Grand Staff and the chapters containing those games.

The study of the staff includes the notes on the staff and one ledger line note in the treble and in the bass. Later games using ledger line staff cards expand this study of the staff.

If your students are studying an instrument which uses only one clef, you may want to familiarize them with the Grand Staff, but concentrate on the one they'll use with their instrument. You may also want to include more notes in the initial study than are shown in the photos. For example, the violin notes:

The games in this chapter use a one-staff board and large notes with letters. Not only does the child hear you refer to a line or a space by letter name, but he can see the note name as well.

Later when the staff cards are used, the alphabet letter is gone and the size of the notes are approaching the size of notes in the music. They also have a stem and look like "real" notes. The alphabet cards are used to help make this transition from notes with letters to staff cards a little smoother.

Learning the staff involves a great deal of memory work. It's strongly suggested that you request daily practice of the staff at home when the children are first learning the names of the notes on the staff. Practicing this only once a week isn't frequent enough.

GAMES FOUND IN THIS CHAPTER

GAME 6—A : *LINES—TREBLE CLEF*

OBJECTIVE : To begin practicing only the line notes of the treble clef. This game follows the same format of 3—G: INTRODUCING THE TREBLE CLEF NOTES, by using the alphabet cards and the notes with letters. If the mothers are present, have them join in the games. This is a great game to do nonverbally.

MATERIALS : 1) Alphabet cards — one set
2) One-staff board
3) Notes with letters
4) Treble clef

PROCEDURE : *STEP ONE:* a) Lay G out on the rug facing the children; b) Add B on top of G; c) Add D; d) Add F, e) Add A; f) Add E below G; g) Add C below E.

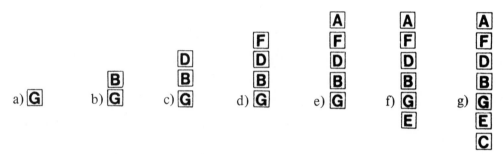

"Would you like to try?" Deal out the cards and let the children line them up on the rug. G should be the first card, then up to A with E and C below G. Repeat this several times.

STEP TWO: Leave the alphabet cards on the floor in one of the patterns shown above. Select the Notes With Letters C E G B D F A (A and C will have ledger lines). Show the children how to put the Notes With Letters on top of the cards. Again, begin with G, up to A, and down to C. Let them do it several times.

STEP THREE: Remove the alphabet cards and place just the notes on the rug in order. Repeat the sequence used before. Let the children try it. Repeat.

STEP FOUR: In this step the children will see how the treble clef tells the names of the lines and place the note pattern they've learned on the staff. Place the one-staff board on the floor in front of the children and let them place the treble clef correctly. Place G on the correct line.

Move the treble clef up one line and place G on the middle line.

Help the children to understand how the position of the treble clef determines the placement of the letter G by moving the clef around.

After returning the treble clef to its usual position, put the notes on the staff in the order used before. Then pass out the notes to the children and let them put them on the staff. This should be easy for them. Repeat many times.

A.M.

STEP FIVE: If you're playing this game nonverbally, it's easy to slide into some mixing and fixing tricks. Snap your fingers to have the children close they're eyes. Switch two of the notes, leaving the others correct. Clap your hands twice for them to open their eyes.

Point to one child who's raised his hand to fix the notes. After he corrects them, give him a sign that you're pleased that he fixed the notes. Repeat, giving everyone a turn.

A variation of this is to turn one note face down while the children close their eyes. After they open their eyes and study the notes, one child can "draw the letter" on the floor with his finger to indicate his answer.

GAME 6—B : *HAND STAFF*

OBJECTIVE : To show the children how they can practice memorizing the staff on their own.

MATERIALS : None

PROCEDURE :   Hold up your hand sideways and spread your fingers apart.

Ask the children to pretend that your five fingers are the five lines of the staff. Point to the fingers in order, naming them. For C and A, you can point to the space below and above your hand. Let the children and parents try this with their own hands, drilling each other.

A.M.

102

"Let's think about all the times we can practice this at home." Let them help you make up a list that could include:

> In the bathtub
> Waiting for breakfast
> While falling asleep at night
> Riding in the car
> Right before practicing
> After dinner
> While standing in lines
> Waiting at traffic lights

By suggesting practicing in this way no one can really give an excuse that they didn't have time or couldn't make up a staff board and notes. This game should simplify practicing as parent and child take 30 seconds here and there to have fun quizzing each other.

GAME 6—C : *TOSS*

OBJECTIVE : To help the children to associate a particular line or space with its letter name.

MATERIALS : 1) One-staff board
2) Clef
3) Toss note
4) Pencil or stick
5) Plastic ledger line sheet

PROCEDURE : Place the staff board in front of the children and let them arrange the clef correctly on the staff. Position the stick or pencil about one foot below the staff board. The children can stand behind the stick and take turns tossing the note.

As a group everyone can name the note together. Soon they'll begin to remember the names of the notes. If you're studying lines and the note lands on a space, simply move it to the nearest line. Use the plastic ledger line sheet for any notes above or below the staff.

GAME 6–D : *PASS OUT*

OBJECTIVE : To help the children associate a particular line or space with its letter name.

MATERIALS : 1) One-staff board
2) Clef
3) Notes with letters

PROCEDURE : Pass out only the notes that the children are learning, as if you were dealing cards. Some children will get one note, others may get two. As soon as they have a note, they can place it on the correct line or space. Let the children check the board after each round to make sure the notes are correct. Saying them together is excellent reinforcement.

If you see a child who is uncertain about where to place a note, help by spelling thirds with him. For the next few rounds, see that the child gets that same note again so he can remember it's placement.

This game is played at a fast pace, dealing out the notes quickly, placing the notes on the staff, saying them together, then quickly dealing out another round of notes.

GAME 6—E : *WHAT NOTE IS MISSING?*

OBJECTIVE : As a variation on PASS OUT, the children guess which one of the notes isn't on the staff.

MATERIALS : 1) One-staff board
2) Clef
3) Notes with letters

PROCEDURE : Use only the notes that the children are learning. Pass out all the notes except one, which you can hide in your hand. After the children have put their notes on the board, let them tell you which note is missing. After naming it correctly, let one child place the note on the staff.

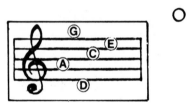

The children think this game is great fun, so it's always a favorite.

GAME 6—F : *ANYTHING WRONG?*

OBJECTIVE : To help children associate a letter name for each line and space.

MATERIALS : 1) One-staff board
2) Clef
3) Notes with letters

PROCEDURE : While the children close their eyes, rearrange the notes on the staff so that some are in the wrong place. When they open their eyes, they can take turns correcting the mistakes.

I find the children keep keenly interested in fixing the notes if each child is allowed to move only one note. Also, everyone is more likely to get a turn on each round.

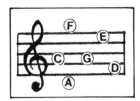

GAME 6—G : *IN THIS ORDER*

OBJECTIVE : To give a child practice in placing all the notes on the staff by himself.

MATERIALS :
1) One-staff board
2) Clef
3) Notes with letters

PROCEDURE : *STEP ONE:* Give all the notes to one child and let him place them on the staff in any sequence. Give each child a turn.

STEP TWO: Line the notes up along the bottom of the staff in a random order, face down. One child is to place these notes on the staff using the notes in order from left to right. If he's uncertain where a particular note belongs, he can count up the staff in thirds. You should help so there's no confusion. Give each child a turn.

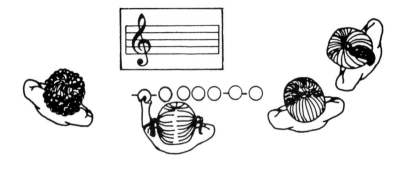

In a later session, when the names of the lines (or spaces) are better known, take each note off the staff after the child places it correctly. This is more of a challenge, since the child doesn't have other notes to relate to.

GAME 6—H   :   *SPACES—TREBLE CLEF*

OBJECTIVE   :   To practice only the spaces of the treble clef. These notes are introduced just like the lines were in 6—A: LINES—TREBLE CLEF and can be memorized using the previous games in this chapter.

MATERIALS :   1)   Alphabet cards — one set
                2)   One-staff board
                3)   Notes with letters
                4)   Treble clef

PROCEDURE :   *STEP ONE:*   Place the staff board on the rug in front of the children and let them put the treble clef on correctly. Place C and E on their correct lines. Ask the children what might be the names of the space between C and E. Because they've played many games with the alphabet cards, they should be able to answer easily that it's D.

STEP TWO: Put the staff board and notes aside. Taking the alphabet cards, place them on the rug in the order shown below beginning with D and on up to B..

Deal out the cards to the children and let them follow the same pattern. Repeat several times.

STEP THREE: Leave the alphabet cards on the rug and pass out the notes with letters D F A C E G to the children and let them place them on top of the alphabet cards. Repeat several times.

STEP FOUR: Remove the alphabet cards and let the children place just the notes with letters on the rug. Repeat several times.

STEP FIVE: Place the staff board in front of the children again and let them place the treble clef in the correct spot. Let them watch as you put the notes on the spaces.

"It's really very easy. You can try." Pass out the

notes to the children and let them place the notes on, in order.

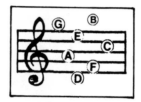

Play many memory games found in this chapter to practice these space notes before you attempt to practice lines and spaces together in the next chapter.

SUGGESTION: To insure that your students practice the lines and/or spaces at home see that each child receives a small book of staff paper with large spaced lines. Ask the parent to draw several rows of notes for the child to identify. Ask them to do this throughout the week and date the assignments. Request that the book be brought to class each week so you can see the books and encourage the children.

NOTE: Help the children recognize that the space B can go either above G or below D.

9
One Clef

Once the children have learned the names of the lines and spaces and played games dealing with either lines or spaces, the next step is to begin playing games using all the notes on that one staff at once. One might think this is an easy progression. However, experience has shown that it can be a little confusing and one should move carefully so the transfer goes easily. Game 7–A: PICK A PAIR was developed for this purpose. It's also helpful to review some of the steps in 3–G: INTRODUCING THE TREBLE CLEF NOTES.

There are many games in this chapter. You may find that it isn't necessary to play all of them when the students are practicing the treble clef. You can save some for when they study the bass clef or for review games.

GAMES FOUND IN THIS CHAPTER

GAME 7—A : *PICK A PAIR*

OBJECTIVE : To show the children how each letter name is found in two different places on the staff. They learn about octaves and how they're positioned on the staff.

MATERIALS :
1) One-staff board
2) Clef
3) Notes With Letters

PROCEDURE : Show the children two G notes. "We all know that one G goes here." Place it on the second line.

"Where does this other G go?" The children should be able to tell you that it goes on the top space. Point out that one of the G's is a line and the other is a space.

Explain that each one of the letters is found in two different places on the staff. We call this an *octave*. They may enjoy discussing the word octave.

"Octaves. *Octa* means eight. Do you know other words that begin with the sound *octa*? How about octopus? Right, an octopus has eight arms. And a stop sign—that's called an octagon. Next time you see a stop sign, count how many sides it has. Anyone know which month begins with the sound *oct*? That's right—it's October. Is that our eighth month?"

"No. It's the tenth month."

"That's interesting, isn't it? Well, we use the ancient Roman calendar and October used to be the eighth month then. But they needed two more months to have the year work out, so two months were named for famous Roman emperors, Julius and Augustus Caesar. What months have their names?"

"July and August."

"Right. That's all the ancient history for today, back to our octaves—notes that are eight notes apart."

Continue through all the octaves so the children can see that each one consists of a line and one a space note. Soon the children will be able to see how far apart on the staff octaves are. This is an important visual concept to learn and will be valuable in sight-reading. It's more beneficial than just counting up eight notes to find the next octave.

To play PICK A PAIR, place the notes in pairs and give one to each child. They can take turns placing their octaves on the staff. Continue for several rounds so everyone has a chance to place several octaves.

GAME 7–B : *PASS OUT*

OBJECTIVE : This game is played just like the game PASS OUT found in the previous chapter, except that all the notes of the staff are passed out.

MATERIALS : 1) One-staff board
2) Clef
3) Notes with letters

PROCEDURE : Place the clef correctly on the staff. Pass out all the notes to the children. They're to put one note on one line or space.

When two children place notes on the same line or space, for example, two E's on the bottom line (treble clef), the child who put his note there first can leave it there. The child with the duplicate note must find the octave.

Let the children check the board after all notes are on.

At a later time, when you think the children really know the names of the notes in the treble clef, you can experiment with a little movable clef game. This clearly shows the children that it's the clef that determines the names of the lines and spaces.

Move the clef up one line so that what's normally the line E now becomes G. Discuss this with the children so they understand what's going on. Play PASS OUT again to let them see if they can put the notes on the correct lines and spaces with the clef low.

The first time we tried this I wasn't certain how it would work, but I was pleasantly surprised to see that they understood the concept. Then I was concerned that they'd be confused as to where the notes really belonged. But again, I was surprised. We moved the clef back into correct position and the notes went on with ease.

This exercise is great preparation before they're introduced to the bass clef.

GAME 7—C   :   *FIX ONE*

OBJECTIVE   :   This game is played like ANYTHING WRONG? found in the previous chapter, except all the notes on the staff are used.

MATERIALS   :   1)   One-staff board
2)   Clef
3)   Notes With Letters

PROCEDURE   :   The children really enjoy this game of detecting errors on the staff. While their eyes are closed, place a majority of the notes incorrectly on the staff. After they open their eyes, they can raise their hands when they find a mistake, taking turns until the whole staff is fixed. The children always look intently so as to be able to find a note to fix.

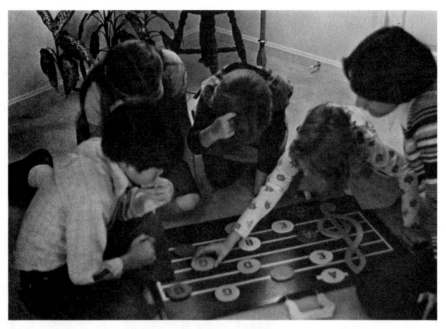

When they correct the last note, be careful not to say, "That's right", but let them look up at you to indicate that they're satisfied they're right. This gives them the chance to check over their work and say the notes again.

GAME 7–D : *MOTHER, FIX IT*

OBJECTIVE : To have fun with Mother while they learn the notes on the staff.

MATERIALS : 1) One-staff board
2) Clef
3) Notes with letters

PROCEDURE : Ask the children, with a tricky look on your face, if they think their mothers know the names of the lines and the spaces. The children will giggle as their mothers roll their eyes and laugh.

Each child can have a turn at this or if you have a large group, two children can work together. Ask one mother to close her eyes while her child scrambles the notes on the staff. The child will be serious in his task and thoughtfully arrange the notes. (I have seen a clever child now and then, who will move the clef sign ever so slightly in hopes of fooling his mother.) The other children will keep careful watch on the mother to make sure she's not peeking.

When the child is finished, have him ask his mother to come over and try to rearrange the notes correctly. This game is most effective if you tip off the mothers in advance to hesitate a little and perhaps even make a few errors. This way, the children really do pay attention and the session continues to be a valuable learning experience for everyone.

"Finished," a mother exclaimed one day.

"Oh, no!" laughed the children. "This one isn't right. It's supposed to go here!" And everyone had a good laugh.

A variation of this game is to let the children try to trick you.

"OK," I said at one lesson. "Who wants to try and trick me?" Everyone raised his hand excitedly. I chose one eager 6 year-old. I could hear the notes being moved around as I covered my eyes.

"Ready! Open your eyes," everyone giggled.

I slowly and thoughtfully corrected the notes, leaving one mistake. "Right. It's all right," the child smiled at me.

"Are you sure?" I asked her.

"Oh dear," she said good naturedly. "I think I tricked myself instead of you!"

GAME 7—E : *WHAT'S RIGHT?*

OBJECTIVE : To ask the children to tell you which notes are right and which are wrong.

MATERIALS : 1) One-staff board
2) Clef
3) Notes with letters

PROCEDURE : While the children's eyes are closed, arrange the notes on the staff. If a small group of three or four are playing, place this number of notes correctly on the board. Place the others incorrectly. If you have a larger group playing, let them take turns.

Ask the children to open their eyes. Explain that many of the notes are wrong. If they can find a correct note, they're to place a finger on it and leave it there until everyone has found one. It's amusing to see arms crisscrossed on the board with children looking in and out to find a right note.

GAME 7–F .	*INTRODUCING STAFF CARDS*
OBJECTIVE :	To help the children get used to identifying notes using the staff cards.
MATERIALS :	1) Staff cards — treble or bass 2) Alphabet cards — two sets
PROCEDURE :	Spread the staff cards in front of the children so they can see what they look like.

Hold them in a pile in your hand. Quickly show one card at a time to the children and let them tell you if it's a line or a space note.

Spread the cards out on the rug and ask if anyone can find the lowest note. Let them line the cards up in order. |

Working together, arrange the alphabet cards under the staff cards.

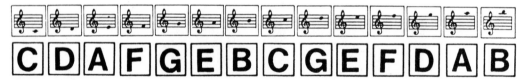

For fun, ask the children to close their eyes. Switch around a few of the alphabet cards.

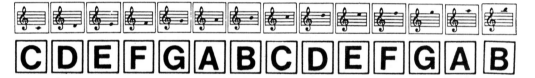

After the children open their eyes, let them take turns moving the staff cards so they're above the proper alphabet card.

Continue to switch cards.

120

GAME 7—G : *MATCH THIS CARD*

OBJECTIVE : The notes on the staff cards are without letters and approaching the size of notes in printed music. To help make the transition from notes with letters smoother, alphabet cards are used with the staff cards.

MATERIALS : 1) Staff cards — one clef
2) Alphabet cards

PROCEDURE : Place several sets of alphabet cards in the middle of the children. Deal out all the staff cards. They're to arrange them in a row in front of themselves and find the matching alphabet cards. It isn't necessary to call attention to any wrong answers. As the game progresses, quietly smile and toss the wrong alphabet card back into the center.

After everyone is finished, collect the staff cards, ask the children to return the alphabet cards to the center and deal out the staff cards again.

GAME 7-H : *MATCH THIS CARD—BACKWARDS*

OBJECTIVE : To practice identifying notes on the staff.

MATERIALS : 1) Staff cards
2) Alphabet cards — several sets

PROCEDURE : This game is like MATCH THIS CARD, except the staff cards are placed on the rug in the center of the children and the alphabet cards are passed out. Be certain to pass out the alphabet cards which will match the staff cards. If you pass out extra alphabet cards, it will be too confusing.

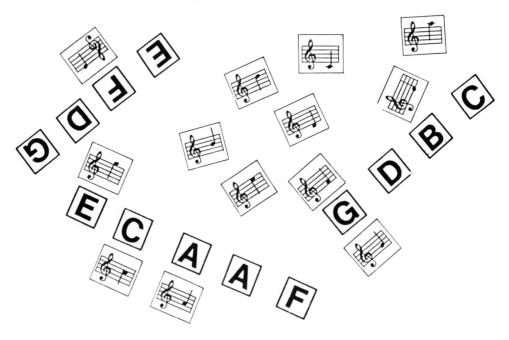

It will be necessary to arrange the staff cards so they aren't on top of one another. Request that the children not move the cards around as they're searching for certain ones. If they do, the card they shove around might be the one that someone is studying. They'll find this version a little tricker than the MATCH THIS CARD.

122

GAME 7–I   :   *LINE 'EM UP*

OBJECTIVE :   To practice naming notes on the staff cards.

MATERIALS :   1)   Staff cards
              2)   Alphabet cards – four sets

PROCEDURE :   This is a good game for just two players. Line the staff cards in a row across the floor. Hand the child two sets of alphabet cards and the mother two sets of alphabet cards. Explain that they're to match the correct alphabet card with the staff card. The child can place his cards below the staff card, face up and the mother can place her cards above the staff card, face down.

     Once they begin, they may work at their own pace. Often the child will work fast so as to try and finish before his mother. When both are finished, you may turn the mother's cards over to see how they match the child's.

VARIATION: This can also be played with two children, or two teams, both placing their cards face down.

GAME 7—J : *USE 'EM UP*

OBJECTIVE : To develop quick name recognition of the notes on the staff cards.

MATERIALS : 1) Staff cards
2) Alphabet cards — several sets

PROCEDURE : Have the children line up the staff cards in a row. Pass out the alphabet cards, giving each child several cards. After you say "go", they can place their alphabet cards under the matching staff cards.

GAME 7—K : *BINGO WITH NAMES*

OBJECTIVE : To practice naming notes on the staff using an ever favorite game, BINGO.

MATERIALS : 1) Bingo cards
2) Bingo dots
3) Alphabet cards — two sets

124

PROCEDURE :   Give each child a bingo card. Taking turns, let each child tell you the names of the notes on his card. Give him four bingo dots. When everyone's ready, place one alphabet card in front of them. If anyone has that note on their card in any octave, they can place a bingo dot over the note.

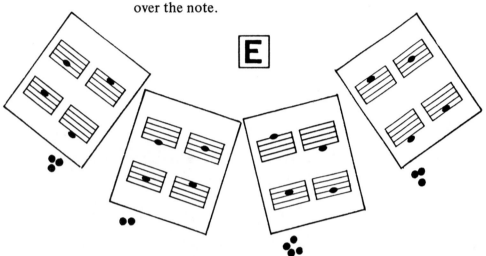

Continue until everyone has filled up their cards. If someone fails to see a note on their card, it isn't necessary to correct them. Most likely they will catch that note when you go through the second set of alphabet cards.

GAME 7—L :   *TOSS*

OBJECTIVE :   To have fun naming notes on the staff.

MATERIALS :
1) One-staff board
2) Toss note
3) Ledger line sheet
4) Pencil or stick

PROCEDURE :   Play this game as described in previous chapters, except let the child who tossed the note name it.

Have the children place the clef sign on the staff. Each child may take a turn standing at the bottom of the staff to toss the note. After a toss, call out whether it landed on a line or a space so there isn't any confusion.

This game can be used for learning notes as well as review for naming the notes.

GAME 7–M : *SHOW ME WITH NAMES*

OBJECTIVE : To practice naming the notes on one staff. This game is designed as review.

MATERIALS : 1) Alphabet cards — one set for each player
2) Staff cards

PROCEDURE : Give each child a set of alphabet cards and keep the staff cards. Select seven cards, each one a different letter of the alphabet. Put the cards in a pile.

Place one staff card in front of the children. They're to look through their cards and find the alphabet card that matches the staff card. Each child is to place this card face down in front of himself.

Continue to place staff cards in a pile, one at a time, allowing time for the children to find the right alphabet card and place it face down on top of their previous card. When you've shown all seven cards, read through your cards together so they can check their cards.

You can also play this game by showing only one staff card and asking the children to place that alphabet card face down. Then call out "show me" and they can turn their cards face up.

GAME 7—N : *RELAY*

OBJECTIVE : To practice naming the notes on the staff.

MATERIALS :
1) Two dictation slates
2) One-staff board and two-staff board — face down
3) Two pennies
4) Alphabet cards — four sets

PROCEDURE : Arrange materials, children and two mothers into two or more teams. Drawing shows one team.

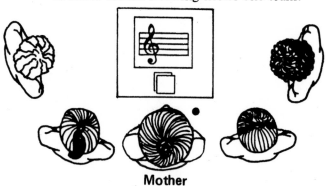

Mother

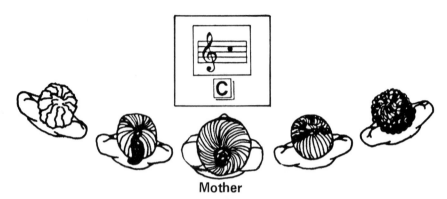

Mother

After you say "go", the mothers can turn over the first alphabet card. The first child on each team is to take the penny (note) and place it correctly on the staff, any octave. The mother turns over another alphabet card and the next child takes the penny and places it on the staff.

The teams can call out "Fine" or any other musical terms they may be learning when they've finished both sets of alphabet cards.

This game can also be played with two pennies per staff. Then the children are to place the pennies in an octave to match the alphabet card.

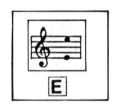

This is a good opportunity for the children to learn the upper or lower space B, if they haven't already.

GAME 7–O   :   *I CAN NAME IT*

OBJECTIVE   :   To practice naming notes on the staff using the staff cards and no alphabet cards.

MATERIALS   :   Staff cards

PROCEDURE : Sit the children on the floor in a circle. Hand one staff card to the child on your left. If he names it correctly, he can keep the card. If not, he's to give it to the person on his left.

Once a card is named correctly, give the next child a new staff card. Continue until all the cards are named.

The children really love this game when they can be the teacher and tell the others if they named the note correctly.

GAME 7–P : *NAME IT*

OBJECTIVE : To name the notes on the staff cards without using the alphabet cards.

MATERIALS : Staff cards

PROCEDURE : Hold up cards for the children to identify. To give this game sparkle, flash the card up for just a second. This really challenges the children to be quick with their eyes and brains.

GAME 7–Q   :   *PAIRS WITH SLATES*

OBJECTIVE   :   To give the children practice naming the notes on the staff without teacher supervision.

MATERIALS   :   1)   Dictation slates
2)   Pennies
3)   Alphabet cards – many sets

PROCEDURE   :   Divide the children into pairs or have a parent play with her child. Give each pair a dictation slate, one penny and two sets of alphabet cards. One person is to turn over the alphabet cards and the other is to put the penny on the right note, any octave. If an error occurs, the person turning the alphabet cards is to help his partner.

When the players have gone through all the alphabet cards, they can be shuffled and the roles switched.

You can also give two pennies to each team, so they can place octaves on the staff instead of single notes.

Each pair of children work independently of the other pairs.

GAME 7—R : *STAFF CARD SNAKES*

OBJECTIVE : To practice naming the notes on the staff cards and have fun with snakes.

MATERIALS : 1) Staff cards — one clef
2) Alphabet cards — several sets

PROCEDURE : Pass out 3—4 sets of alphabet cards to the children and let them make either a thirds snake or a regular alphabet snake.

After they've done this once, toss in the staff cards as you deal out the alphabet cards. Explain that every few cards they can use a staff card to fit into the snake. Let them do the snake by themselves.

Depending on which staff cards you have, you may need to toss in a few extra alphabet cards so the snake works out. Try this snake by yourself once and you'll see what alphabet cards to add.

GAME 7–S : *NO CLEF*

OBJECTIVE : To practice naming notes without a clef sign on the card. In printed music, the clef is found only at the beginning of the staff so children should practice notes without a clef sign next to the note. Although they won't see it, they can imagine it being there.

MATERIALS : 1) Clefless staff cards
2) Alphabet cards

PROCEDURE : These cards can be used with alphabet cards to play any of the games found in this chapter. They can also be played in combination with regular staff cards.

     Each card has a dot which should be turned so it's in the lower left hand corner. Otherwise, there'll be notes duplicated.

GAME 7–T : *LINES–BASS CLEF*

OBJECTIVE : Once the students have learned the notes in the treble clef and practiced both the lines and spaces together, they can be introduced to the bass clef. If the treble clef notes are learned thoroughly, it will be relatively easy to learn the bass clef. Even students who may only need one clef to read the music from their instrument, should be familiar with the other clef.

MATERIALS : 1) One-staff board
2) Notes with letters
3) Bass clef
4) Treble clef

132

PROCEDURE : Place the one staff board in front of the children and let them place the treble clef correctly. Pass out the line notes for the treble clef (-C-, E, G, B, D, F, -A-) and ask the children to put the notes on the correct lines.

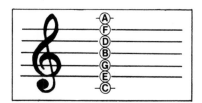

Collect the notes off the staff but before passing them out again, move the treble clef so it's one line lower than before. Pass out the notes and ask the children to place them correctly.

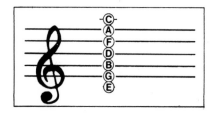

Repeat this once more with the clef remaining in the low position.

"This E could use some ledger lines, couldn't it? And since this A's on a line, we can trade it in for a regular note, right? OK, let's play Pass Out with these notes once." Pass out the notes and let the students put them on the correct lines.

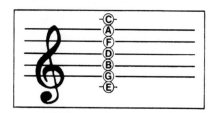

"I have a surprise for you. You just showed me that you know your bass clef lines!" With a smile of congratulations upon your face, switch the treble clef with the bass clef. "How smart you are!"

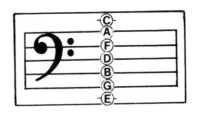

"And it checks out. The F is just in the right place, right between the two dots."

"Is that really the bass clef lines?" they'll ask.

"That's it," you can assure them. Play Pass Out a few more times.

PRACTICE THE NAMES OF THE BASS CLEF LINES WITH THE CHILDREN BY PLAYING THE GAMES FOUND IN CHAPTER 8. YOU MIGHT ENJOY MAKING UP A FEW OF YOUR OWN!

GAME 7—U : *SPACES—BASS CLEF*

OBJECTIVE : Once the students really know their lines on the bass clef, you can begin on the spaces. This can be done in the same steps used to learn the spaces in the treble clef. These are illustrated below. The games in Chapter 8 will help them memorize the spaces.

MATERIALS : 1) Alphabet cards — one set
2) Notes With Letters
3) One-staff board
4) Bass clef

PROCEDURE :

STEP ONE: **STEP TWO:**   **STEP THREE:**

B
G
E
C
A
F
D

B
G
E
C
A
F
D

B
G
E
C
A
F
D

STEP FOUR:

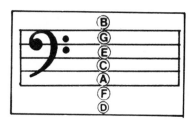

GAME 7–V   :   *LINES AND SPACES—BASS CLEF*

OBJECTIVE   :   After the students have memorized the lines and memorized the spaces and played the games in Chapter VIII
using the bass clef, they can play the games in this
chapter to practice both the lines and spaces together.
Begin with PICK A PAIR and progress on to other
favorites.

MATERIALS   :   See each game

PROCEDURE   :   See each game

GAME 7—W : *NAME THAT NOTE*

OBJECTIVE : NAME THAT NOTE is designed to give students an enjoyable opportunity to practice naming notes on the treble and bass clefs. The board is arranged with the notes appearing in steps, simple skips or octaves so play is not too difficult. Being able to play this game is a good preview for Musopoly.

MATERIALS :
1) NAME THAT NOTE board
2) Treble clef and bass clef cards
3) Alphabet people
4) Large dice
5) Pennies
6) Gold coins

PROCEDURE : Before playing, students should study and know their notes well. Use one board with 2—6 players. If there are more players, use 2 boards. This game may last one theory class or any amount of time required or desired.

10
Signs and Symbols

In helping parents to acquire this refined skill of reading music, I've become impressed with how carefully we all must watch for each little dot or line and never overlook anything. How often a mother has said to me . . . "You mean that little line there changes the notes that much?"

When presented carefully, the students can have fun learning the music symbols found on nearly every page of music. Although some of the words are difficult for the young ones to say; their later studies will come much easier because they learned about the various signs and symbols. *It's important for children to have experienced the sign in their playing before learning it in class.* Otherwise, they're merely memorizing definitions.

"You know, my son has become so interested in the music book lately. Whenever we begin a new song, he sits down with the book and studies the music to look for fermatas, tenutos, staccatos, and repeat signs. I think Da Capo is his favorite. I'm so impressed with his interest."

Students reading their pieces from the music are so careful to observe each dot, rest, and dynamic marking. There's nothing sloplly about their reading, because they know what everything means.

GAMES FOUND IN THIS CHAPTER

GAME 8—A . *DYNAMICS*

OBJECTIVE . To learn the names pp, p, mp, mf, f, ff, how to recognize them, and what they mean. Depending on the age of the children, these signs can be introduced by twos or all in one session.

MATERIALS : Orange cards

PROCEDURE : *STEP ONE:* This step is best done without any visual reinforcement. It's purpose is to teach meanings and pronunciations of pp, p, mp, mf, f, and ff. It's a popular, fun and easy game.

With the children sitting before you on the floor, call out "FORTE" in a loud voice. Motion for them to say "FORTE" back to you. Surprised at your loud voice, they might be too soft, so call out "FORTE" again and let them yell "FORTE" back to you.

Say "piano" softly, then pause for them to say "piano". Repeat the words several times.

"FORTE" you call out, smiling.
"FORTE" they answer.
"piano" you whisper.
"piano" they whisper back.

Add the other words in this session or another session, depending on the age of your students. From experience, I've learned that the children will learn to pronounce fortissimo and pianissimo easily if you streatch out the first syllables a little as you say the words. Fooorrrrtissimo. Piiiiaaaanissimo.

STEP TWO: (Note: Although the drawing shows a child facing sideways, then frontwards, have the children face you the whole time.)

pp   p   ᵐp   ᵐf   f   ff

Motioning to the children to follow you, fold yourself into a ball on the floor as shown in the drawing for pianissimo. Once everyone's joined you, whisper "pianissimo" together.

Move to the next position and say "piano" softly together. Each time go back to PP and add one more dynamic level until you've said all six words in order. It's great fun to have everyone in the room join you in this game and to go from soft to loud as described as well as backwards from FF to PP.

STEP THREE: Tell the children, "We're looking for these six cards. One will have the letter "P" on it and another one will have the letter "F" on it. There'll also be cards with two ff's, two pp's, and mp and an mf card. Look closely and call out "STOP" when you see any of them.

Hold *all the orange cards* in your hands. Quickly toss the cards down one at a time in front of the children, *placing them in one pile.* (Going through the cards this way gives the children a glimpse, even if only briefly, of the other orange cards they're going to be learning.) The children will watch intensely for the correct cards to be tossed down.

"STOP! . . . STOP!!" they'll call out as they see the letters. As the children identify these cards, separate them from the pile. After the six dynamic cards have been found, set the other orange cards aside.

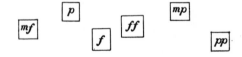

"Good, you spotted the cards easily." Pointing to the P card tell the children . . . "this card means to play softly. The P stands for the word piano. Piano means soft in Italian. You see, several hundred years ago there were many important composers writing great music. Many of these men lived in Italy, a country in southern Europe. They used Italian words in their music and we continue to use them even today." Explain the other cards.

"Anyone have an idea which of these cards stands for the word forte?" Chances are that they'll choose the right card.

$$\boxed{f}$$

"How about piano?"

$$\boxed{p} \qquad \boxed{f}$$

"Which one looks like fortissimo?"

$$\boxed{p} \qquad \boxed{f} \; \boxed{ff}$$

"Pianissimo?"

$$\boxed{pp} \; \boxed{p} \qquad \boxed{f} \; \boxed{ff}$$

"These two left must be MEZZO (pronounced metzo), PIANO and one is Mezzoforte." It's fun to play a little trick. "Are they in the right spot?"

$$\boxed{pp} \; \boxed{p} \; \boxed{mf} \; \boxed{mp} \; \boxed{f} \; \boxed{ff}$$

"No! . . . this way," they'll correct you.

$$\boxed{pp} \; \boxed{p} \; \boxed{mp} \; \boxed{mf} \; \boxed{f} \; \boxed{ff}$$

"Very good. You know all of them." Practice saying all the cards several times with the children.

STEP FOUR: Holding the cards in your hand so the children can't see them, let each child take a turn drawing one card and telling you the Italian names and what they mean. Help them to answer correctly if they hesitate.

Besides saying the words, the children may enjoy getting into the correct body position to match the card they draw.

GAME 8-B   :   *DYNAMIC MIX-UP*

OBJECTIVE   :   To help the children memorize dynamic signs and their meaning.

MATERIALS :   Orange cards — pp, p, mp, mf, f, ff

PROCEDURE :   Have the children lay out the dynamic cards in order.

"Close your eyes and I'm going to mix things up." Switch the cards around and when the children open their eyes, let them take turns putting the cards back in the right order. You'll find the children enjoy doing this over and over.

To give this game a different twist, request that the children only move one card as they fix up the cards. They should also try and leave the six places intact as they move the cards. This way, everyone stays interested throughout the game. Sample steps:

1. | mp | pp | mf | p | f | ff |

2. | pp | mp | p | f | ff |

3. | pp | | mp | p | f | ff |

4. | pp | p | mp | | f | ff |

5. | pp | p | mp | mf | f | ff |

Adding body movements to this makes it even more fun.

GAME 8–C	:	*CRESCENDO AND DECRESCENDO*
OBJECTIVE	:	To teach the children about Crescendo and Decrescendo.
MATERIALS	:	1) Orange cards: 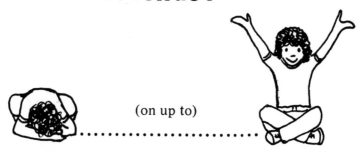
PROCEDURE	:	Holding one of the cards for the children, ask: "Pretend that there is sound inside these two lines. At this end the sound would be small because there isn't much space between the lines. But at this end the space is wider, so the sound can be louder." Point with your fingers.

"We call this a crescendo: gradually getting louder and louder." Let them practice the word.

The children will learn the meaning easily if you act it out:

Crescendo!

(on up to)

Decrescendo can be introduced in the same manner. Help the children to pronounce the word "day-crescendo."

Decrescendo!

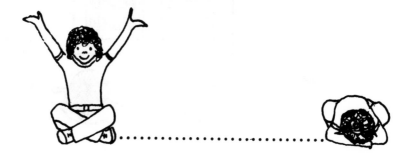

GAME 8–D : *FOLLOW THAT SIGN*

OBJECTIVE : To learn Da Capo, fine and repeat signs.

MATERIALS : 1) Orange cards – D.C., Fine, $\lVert\colon \quad \colon\rVert$
2) One alphabet person
3) The music book

PROCEDURE : *DA CAPO and FINE:* Show the children the D.C. card and explain that this is usually found at the end of a piece of music. Open the music in front of them.

"I'm going to turn the pages. Stop me when you see a Da Capo marking in the music." They'll study the music intently and pounce on the page where the first D.C. occurs.

Taking the alphabet person, trace him along each line of music. When he comes to the end, at the D.C., take him back to the beginning. Explain that D.C. is an abbreviation for the Italian words Da Capo which means to return to the beginning of the music. Capo means *head*, and the beginning is the "head" of the music.

Follow the music until Fine occurs, explaining that "fine" means *the end* or *the finish* of the piece of music.

Find other songs with D.C. and let the children practice tracing through the music using the alphabet person.

Da Capo and Fine Signs

144

REPEAT SIGNS: You can let the alphabet person "glide" through the music to demonstrate how repeat signs work. Explain how repeat signs aren't written at the beginning of the music. Let the children find pieces using repeat signs and then trace through them with the alphabet person.

When we come upon a repeat sign, everyone says "Ping" in a high voice, and back goes the alphabet person. When we come upon that same repeat sign again, no one says "ping" since we only repeat once.

If the children know how the piece sounds, it's helpful to have them sing along as the alphabet person traces through the music. This enables them to "hear" the repeats.

Repeat Signs

GAME 8—E : *SHARPS AND FLATS*

OBJECTIVE : To teach the half-step whole-step concept, the meaning of sharps, flats, and natural signs and their relation on the keyboard.

MATERIALS : 1) Orange cards — sharps ♯ , flats ♭ , naturals ♮
2) Stairs (if you have them)

PROCEDURE : *STEP ONE:* Half and whole-steps can be clearly demonstrated with ordinary walking. Line up the children so that they can see you. Explain that we can call regular walking whole-steps. If we take little steps, keeping our shoes touching, we can call these half-steps.

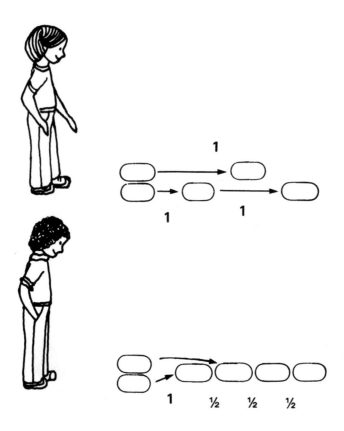

The children will have a great time if you play a game like "red light—green light" and call out half-steps and whole-steps for them to walk.

STEP TWO: Explain that sharps and flats are half-steps up and down. Sharps go *up* and flats, like a flat tire, go *down*.

If you have stairs in or near your studio or classroom, they'll help the students really grasp the concept of up for sharps and down for flats. If there're no stairs available, use the level floor, forwards for sharps, and backwards for flats.

146

Position the children at the foot of the stairs and yourself at or near the top. If you hold up the sharp card, they're to step up one step on the stairs, a half-step. Explain that a whole-step would be two steps.

If you hold a flat card up, they're to step back down one step. Everyone smiles and giggles, but will really remember what sharps and flats are as they inch up and down the stairs.

STEP THREE: An important part of this game is relating the concept of sharps and flats to the keyboard (and their own instruments, if they're studying other than the piano). Play one note on the piano and explain that just like the steps they walked, a half-step from any note is just one note away.

Place an alphabet person on one key, let's say it's C. Point out C♯ and C♭. Do this with several other keys. By learning sharps and flats in this manner, the children haven't been incorrectly taught that sharps and flats are only the black notes on the piano. They can know that many times sharps and flats are black notes.

Let the children play sharps and flats around many notes. You can explain that a natural sign means to *cancel* the sharp or flat. It's also used to indicate white keys, e.g. C natural, F natural, etc.

STEP FOUR: Place the music book in front of the children and let them find sharps, flats and naturals in the music. Discuss that they always appear before the note, apply to all of those notes in the measure (only the one note though, not other octaves), and end with the bar line. Discuss briefly how key signatures work and what they mean.

GAME 8—F   :   *LEARNING THE OTHERS*

OBJECTIVE   :   To learn names and definitions of other symbols and how they're found in the music.

MATERIALS   :   Orange cards and the music book

PROCEDURE   :   After the children experience other symbols in their playing, you can show them the different orange cards and teach the definitions. It'll be much more meaningful for a child to study a term like "a tempo" after he has played a piece that has a ritard followed by a tempo. Otherwise, he may merely memorize the definition and not really understand it. If terms are taught too early, you may find that the children have trouble remembering them.

148

A.M.

It's advisable to use the music as well as the cards as the children learn the symbols. First, show the card and talk about its meaning, then let the children find it in the music book. If you can think of ways to illustrate the symbols as was done with the dynamic signs, the children will remember them easier.

For example: To illustrate ritard, you could have everyone walking across the room. Call out "ritard" and they should begin to get slower and finally stop. Or after calling "ritard", call out "a tempo" before they slow down completely. They should begin walking normally again.

Here are some suggestions for brief definitions that the children can understand:

pp	pianissimo	Very soft
p	piano	Soft
mp	mezzopiano	Medium soft
mf	mezzoforte	Medium loud
f	forte	Loud
ff	fortissimo	Very loud
	Da Capo	Go back to the beginning and play until fine
Fine	fine	End or finish
𝄆 𝄇	repeat signs	Play that section of music again
rit.	ritardando	To gradually get slower

a tempo	a tempo	Return to the normal speed
0 1 2 3 4 5	finger numbers	Demonstrate with your finger
♭	flat	Down a half-step
♯	sharp	Up a half-step
♮	natural	Cancel the sharp or flat
8va	octava	An octave higher or lower
	staccato	A short note
	accent	To stress the note
	tenuto	Play the note exactly as written
	fermata	Hold the note longer
	trill	Demonstrate with two fingers
	appogiatura	The little note is played on the beat
	acciaccatura	Grace note—the little note is played quickly before the beat
	staff	Lines and spaces on which music is written
	bar line	A line dividing measures
	slur	Notes connected together and played legato

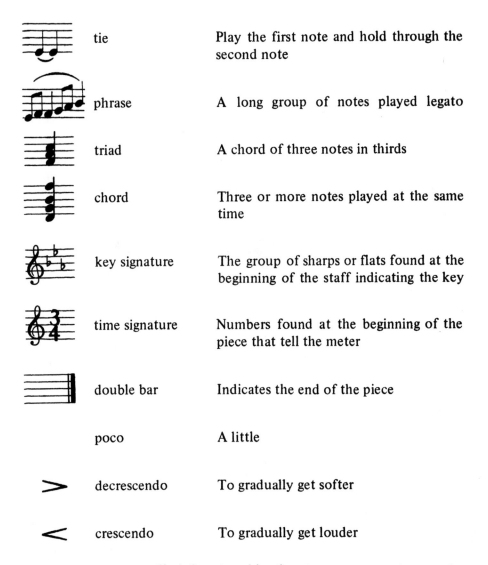 tie	tie	Play the first note and hold through the second note
	phrase	A long group of notes played legato
	triad	A chord of three notes in thirds
	chord	Three or more notes played at the same time
	key signature	The group of sharps or flats found at the beginning of the staff indicating the key
	time signature	Numbers found at the beginning of the piece that tell the meter
	double bar	Indicates the end of the piece
	poco	A little
	decrescendo	To gradually get softer
	crescendo	To gradually get louder

Feel free to add other terms you want your students to know.

GAME 8—G	**:**	*PASS AROUND AND ACT OUT*
OBJECTIVE	**:**	To have fun reinforcing the meanings.
MATERIALS	**:**	Orange Cards — whichever ones you've studied
PROCEDURE	**:**	This game is silly, fun and bound to bring laughter to your class as the children internalize the meanings of

various symbols.

Select one card, we'll use fermata as our example. Handing the card to the student on one side of you, say:

"FFFFFFEEEEERRRRMMMMAAAATTTTAAAA."

At the same time draw a half circle in front of his face, pull your hand back towards you, then reach out and "dot" his nose.

He then turns to the person on his side and repeats what you did. So the motion is passed around the circle.

Feel free to make up your own descriptive motions or let the children improvise. Some suggestions:

STACCATO: While passing the card, say staccato in a quick manner and bounce one finger off the persons knee.

DOUBLE BAR LINE: While passing the card and saying double bar, use your second and third fingers to draw lines a few inches in front of the person's body.

ACCENT: Hand the card to the person. While hitting a fist into your other hand, say accent sharply.

Good luck with your ideas!

GAME 8—H : *WHAT CAN YOU FIND?*

OBJECTIVE : To practice spotting the symbols in the music.

MATERIALS : Music books

PROCEDURE : Open the music and let the children call out symbols and signs as they see them. It's good to use even advanced music so they can see that all types of music use the same symbols. Your students might sound like this:

"I see a treble clef *and* a bass clef."

"There's a forte, there's another, and another . . ."

"I see a pianissimo with a decrescendo."

"So far, I've counted 17 sharps!"

"Da Capo! Da Capo! Right here!"

GAME 8–I : *I SEE . . .*

OBJECTIVE : To practice recognizing terms and verbalizing their definitions.

MATERIALS : Orange cards

PROCEDURE : *STEP ONE:* Lay out, face up, all the orange cards the children have learned. Go around the circle giving each child a turn.

"Pauline, I see a card that means to play very softly." Pauline looks over the cards, finds pianissimo, says it for you and turns the card face down.

"Dick, I see a card that means to slow down gradually."

"Oh, ritard," says Dick and turns the card face down. And so the game continues until all the cards are turned over.

STEP TWO: This is played the same way, except the children give you a definition. Then you give the name, find the card and turn it over. This is more challenging since the children must give the definition.

GAME 8—J　　:　*THE BIG PYRAMID (based on a famous T.V. program)*

OBJECTIVE　:　To have fun giving definitions of orange cards.

MATERIALS　:　Orange cards

PROCEDURE　:　Divide the children into pairs or have a parent play with a child. Give one person from each pair four orange cards. That person is to describe or demonstrate each card one at a time for his partner. The partner is to name the symbol and then receive the card.

When all four cards have changed hands, they're to be returned to you in exchange for four new orange cards. The opposite person defines the cards this time.

Everyone plays at the same time, there's no time limit and of course, no $25,000 in prizes.

GAME 8—K.　:　*WHAT CAN YOU HEAR?*

OBJECTIVE　:　To give the children experience in listening for staccatos, accents and other orange cards.

154

MATERIALS : 1) The children's instruments
2) Orange cards

PROCEDURE : Lay out the orange cards, face up, in the middle of the children. Select one child to play a piece on his instrument. Explain to the remaining children that they're to listen to the performance and pick up orange cards as they hear or see them in the playing.

After the piece is finished, the children can take turns explaining which signs and symbols they picked up. Let other children be the performers.

GAME 8–L : *MATCH A SYMBOL*

OBJECTIVE : To familiarize the children with how these symbol words are spelled. (For older children.)

MATERIALS : 1) Orange cards
2) Word cards

PROCEDURE : Arrange the orange cards in the center of the children, face up. Pass out all the word cards. The children are to select the orange cards which match their word cards. They can check their answers, since the symbols are on the back of the word cards.

A.M.

GAME 8—M : *LEARNING TEMPOS*

OBJECTIVE : To teach the different tempo markings and their relationship to one another. I'm always surprised at how quickly and easily children can learn these terms. They're best introduced after the children have been playing and listening to lots of music in different tempos for a *long time*.

MATERIALS : Yellow tempo cards

PROCEDURE : *STEP ONE:* Take a few moments of *several* class sessions and say the various tempo words, letting the children say them back to you, before they see how the words are pronounced. If they see the words first, they may have trouble with correct pronunciations. Remember—say it first, then read it.

STEP TWO: "I've some new cards to show you today. These are tempo markings which tell you how fast or how slow to play a certain piece of music. Let's sing a little of *Twinkle Twinkle Little Star,* **very** slowly. Twinkle . . ."

"Almost puts you to sleep! Medium tempo—Twinkle . . ."

"Easier, right? Now, very fast—Twinkle, twinkle . . ."

During this session it'll probably be best if you teach just three tempos: largo, moderato and prestissimo. The children will understand. if you talk about largo being very slow, moderato as a medium tempo, and prestissimo very fast.

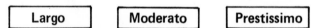

Hold the cards up in front of the children so one card shows at a time. "I'm going to show you one card at a time. Call out the name of the card when you see one we learned today."

This is easy for them and good reinforcement.

STEP THREE: You can choose to learn several more tempos in following classes, or all at once, depending on your students. This is the order I suggest the cards be presented.

1	2	3	4	5
Largo	Largo	Largo	Largo	Largo
	Lento	Lento	Lento	Lento
		Adagio	Adagio	Adagio
			Andante	Andante
				Andantino
Moderato	Moderato	Moderato	Moderato	Moderato
				Allegretto
			Allegro	Allegro
		Vivace	Vivace	Vivace
	Presto	Presto	Presto	Presto
Prestissimo	Prestissimo	Prestissimo	Prestissimo	Prestissimo

STEP FOUR: Lay the cards out one at a time, left to right, saying the words as you do. With each word, you could take the song, Twinkle, and sing a phrase in the appropriate tempo.

Your cards should end up in this order: largo, lento, adagio, andante, andantino, moderato, allegretto, allegro, vivace, presto, prestissimo.

(NOTE: I used the *Harvard Dictionary*; Brye, *Basic Principles of Music Theory*; a little pocket dictionary; and my metronome for this order. There are certainly other markings such as "agitato" and "grave" but in checking, I didn't find these to be tempos, but more a feeling of mood. Also, vivace and presto are very close in meaning.)

To give the children a more concrete relationship for the different tempos, you can all move your arms like trains. Starting with lento, everyone can move their arms very slowly. As you call out the tempos together, gradually move your arms faster until at prestissimo, everyone is moving like crazy!

"Next time your Mom mentions about cleaning up your room, be sure to do it presto and not lento . . . "

We also talk about prestissimo being as fast as you can play your piece **well**.

GAME 8–N	:	*TEMPO MIX-UP*
OBJECTIVE	:	To memorize the order of the tempos.
MATERIALS	:	Yellow tempo cards
PROCEDURE	:	Lay out the cards, in order, and let the children study them for a moment. Ask everyone to close their eyes.

"I'm mixing the cards up. After I tell you to open your eyes, please raise your hand if you see something wrong. Remember that you can only move one card at a time, even if you have to put a card on top of another one. On a later turn, someone can slide that card out from under the other one and place it correctly."

Ask the children to open their eyes. Call on them one at a time to fix the cards. This is a lot of fun and good for learning.

GAME 8—O : *TEMPO PASS-OUT*

OBJECTIVE : To memorize the order of the tempos.

MATERIALS : Yellow tempo cards

PROCEDURE : Pass out the cards to the children and let them put them out, in order, like a snake. The child with the "largo" card will put it out first, to the left, and then the rest in order. Let the children do this without your assistance and correct their own mistakes.

Feel free to make up other games for these cards.

GAME 8—P : *TEMPOS IN THE MUSIC*

OBJECTIVE : To relate the tempo markings to the music books.

MATERIALS : Music books

PROCEDURE : Using music that they've already played, show the children how the tempo marking is found at the beginning of the piece opposite the composer's name. Turn the pages slowly for them, letting them call out the tempos of their pieces and discuss how fast or slow the piece is to be.

Later, do this with other music as well.

A.M.

11
Musopoly

There's only one game in this chapter and it's guaranteed to be a winner with your students. Pronounced Mus (like mus-ic) op - o - ly, the game borrows the thrills and challenges for that popular American real estate trading game, but none of its details.

Designed not so much to teach, but to reinforce concepts and facts learned in the preceeding chapters, the game should be played without teacher or parental interference once the rules are explained.

MUSOPOLY is available in its own pattern, MUSIC 19 #1906 which includes:

1. MUSOPOLY game printed full size 30″ x 30″
2. A complete rule sheet
3. Directions for coloring and backing the game
4. Directions for making the accessories

SHOWN BELOW: finished game made from pattern.

A.M.

GAME 9—A : *MUSOPOLY*

OBJECTIVE : This game is designed to be used as reinforcement for concepts that the children have learned by playing the games up to this point in the book. I suppose the real objective is merely to have fun with the fundamentals of music. Without a doubt, that objective is always met. Since I've made up this game, not a week has gone by without several students begging to play it during theory class.

MATERIALS :
1) MUSOPOLY board
2) Pink chance cards
3) Box of pennies
4) Alphabet people
5) Staff cards
6) Orange symbol cards
7) Blue jello sticks *or* rhythm cards and boards
8) Word cards (optional)
9) Gold coins *or* other play money
10) Large dice

PROCEDURE : During the game, the players can win money for naming notes in the treble and bass clef, defining the orange (symbol) cards, clapping rhythms, performing solos and answering questions about music and their instrument. The game is versatile and can be used with many levels of musical abilities.

TO SET UP THE BOARD:

Bass and Treble clef staff cards, Orange cards, and Pink chance cards are placed face down on the corresponding color squares in the middle of the board.

A rhythm is written out with the blue jello sticks.

BEFORE PLAYING:

Two players are chosen to be bankers, one for gold coins and one for pennies.

Each player selects an alphabet person to use in play.

Each player receives 5 pennies.

TO PLAY:

On a roll of the dice a player moves the number of spaces in the direction of the arrow. If he lands on a treble clef space, he draws a treble clef card and names the note. If he lands on a bass clef card he names the note. When a player lands on an orange sharp, he draws the top orange card and defines and names the card. Pink question mark spaces indicate various challenges and questions. Examples:

Which is faster — lento or presto?
Will you bow correctly?
Give players next to you one penny each.
Move ahead one fifth.
Free!! Two pennies.
If you practiced today, take an extra turn.

For answering any of the cards correctly the player wins a penny.

There are also spaces marked for playing a polished piece with the option of winning 3 pennies or a gold coin. There are four spaces which indicate the player should clap the rhythm. And two corner spaces which say "Give one penny to every player" and "Collect one penny from every player."

There are various other little rules to further challenge the players and bring excitement to the game.

Nothing on the board is bought, there's no jail, and no one is ever forced out of the game for lack of money—the bank is very generous . . .

The game is over when time is called, usually at the end of theory class. The players enjoy the spirit of the game and don't make much fuss about who has collected the most money.

If you've a large group of students, two Musopoly games can be going on at one time.

A.M.

12
Play It Again –
Dictation

Reading music depends on more than just the ability to recognize the names of notes. The children must begin relating notes to one another.

Much melodic material moves in steps or small skips. If the child can "hear" some of these patterns of steps and skips and write them correctly on the staff, he'll be developing a most valuable concept.

What a help it'll be in reading music, to be able to look at a phrase of notes and have a good idea how it sounds even *before* playing it.

In the beginning, the dictation exercises can begin on the line G in the treble clef, since the G 5-note scale fits within the staff and uses no accidentals. Later, other starting notes should be used, as well as the bass clef.

Take special note of the last games using song puzzle cards. With these early dictation games the patterns are played without rhythm patterns. This can be introduced later.

GAMES FOUND IN THIS CHAPTER

GAME 10—A :   *INTRODUCING DICTATION*

OBJECTIVE   :   To introduce melodic dictation and develop the children's abilities to hear simple number patterns played
on the piano. I use middle C as the starting note, since
it's an easy range for the children to sing in, and there
are only white notes in the 5-note scales.

MATERIALS :   Piano

PROCEDURE :   Before having the children write out number patterns
themselves, it's helpful to practice hearing patterns as
a group for a number of sessions. Your initial explanation could go like this:

"I'd like to do some melodic dictation with you
today. Dictation is hearing music and being able to say
what was played. First, we'll try it with numbers."

Play five step-wise notes, such as C D E F G, on
the piano. "That was five different notes, so the numbers would be 1 2 3 4 5." Play the notes again and say
the numbers with them. Play other simple patterns using
1 2 3 4 5 and call out the numbers the second time you
play the pattern. As the children understand the concept, they'll begin saying the numbers with you.

In the beginning you needn't discourage them
from watching your fingers since this will aid them in
understanding the concept.

Suggest that when they don't need to watch, you'd
prefer they look away, only using their ears.

To help train their memories, explain that they're
to listen with their eyes closed while you play a pattern
of notes two times. (You may suggest that the first time
they can listen to the pattern, the second time try to
play it with their right hand on the rug.) Then they can
open their eyes and sing the numbers.

"I know it may seem easy to sing these patterns
as soon as you hear them, but I want you to wait until
I'm completely finished with both playings. Someday,
we'll be writing longer melodies and this will prepare
you to be able to do that well."

Always play the patterns slowly (approximately
one note per second), clearly and evenly. Progress
only as the children are able to answer with ease.

You may find that between 5 and 10 patterns in one session is good. Again, it's the number of different times you do this, not the length of each session. With practice, the children should be able to sing back simple patterns of five different step-wise pitches.

GAME 10–B	:	*DICTATION WITH NUMBERS*
OBJECTIVE	:	To teach the children how to write down simple number patterns. This game can be played after the children have had lots of practice singing back number patterns as a group.
MATERIALS	:	1) Piano 2) Dictation slates and pencils
PROCEDURE	:	Give each child a number slate. Before asking them to write out patterns after they hear them, just give them some simple number patterns to write.

"I'm going to call out some numbers. Wait until I call out the whole pattern and then see if you can write it." Samples could be 12345, 12321, 1234543, 1212 345, 1122345.

After playing a few number patterns for them to sing back to you, let them try writing numbers of what they hear. As in the previous game, ask them to close their eyes while you play the pattern two times. The first is to get an idea of what the pattern is and the second is to try and think the numbers (and possibly finger along) as it's played. Then they can open their eyes and write what you played.

As they finish writing, they can hold up their slates for you to see.

If the pattern isn't correct, quietly shake your head a little and the child can try again. Perhaps, another hearing will help him to correct his work and let others check theirs.

As you work with the children, you'll be able to judge what kind of patterns to play. Remember, that the children will always try their best and succeed more if you progress in small steps with plenty of repetition. Measure the difficulty of the patterns so they can write them out correctly after one or two playings. If they make errors or ask you to keep playing it, your patterns are either too complicated or too long. Beginning patterns could be:

111	11223	123123	12123	1321
1111	12333	12312	123231	13231
1122	12121	12321	13131	1213
1211	112233	1232	13123	132321
112211	12111	123211	13211	12321

If they get a sampling of these with ease, add the numbers 4 and/or 5 to their patterns. Progress in small steps.

GAME 10–C : *DICTATION WITH NOTES*

OBJECTIVE : To take melodic dictation using the staff. Play this once the children are doing the previous games easily.

MATERIALS : 1) Dictation slates and notes (pennies)
2) Piano

PROCEDURE : When giving melodic dictation, you can use the G above middle C as the starting note since there are no sharps or flats involved in the five-note scale. It also fits comfortably in the middle of the staff.

Each child should receive a dictation slate and nine or ten pennies. Tell the children that the first note will be G and let them place their pennies on that line.

During the first session(s) with the staff slates, merely call out number patterns for them to write. Keep one staff for yourself. As the children are writing out a pattern, write it on your own staff. They can easily check theirs against yours. This is better than having to single out a child who may have a little trouble at first. Help them gently, if necessary.

Since everyone is used to writing in one dimension, writing on a staff which is two dimensions, may take a bit of practice. Common things to watch for are children who think they should use only the lines—pattern given was 12345:

Descending patterns may end up looking like this for 123454321:

Help them not to put pennies underneath each other if you're playing a melody of 123451:

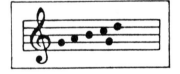

When they're used to the staff, you can play patterns for them to write. As before, ask them to close their eyes and listen to the entire pattern played twice before writing anything on their slates. Before playing a pattern, you should wait until everyone has one penny on G, is quiet and has their eyes closed.

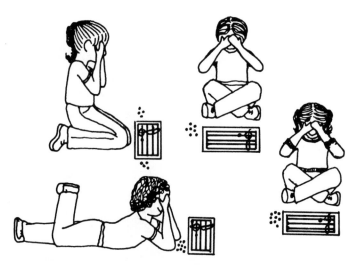

After they have all written the pattern on their slates, it's fun to sing the patterns by note name or number name together. It's also good practice for naming the lines and spaces.

GAME 10–D : *PUT YOUR FINGER ON IT*

OBJECTIVE : To introduce skips in dictation patterns.

MATERIALS : 1) Dictation slates and pennies
2) Piano

PROCEDURE : Ask the children to lay out the notes shown below, on their staffs.

Explain that you're going to play this pattern, but leave out one of the notes. As you play, they can follow along with their finger. When they hear the note that was left out, they can put their finger on it. They should be able to hear which note was missing in one hearing.

When one note becomes easy to find, leave out two notes. Later they may be able to hear the whole pattern, then go back and put their finger on the note. You can also ask them to find a missing note from:

GAME 10—E : *HEAR ANY THIRDS?*

OBJECTIVE : To develop the children's ability to hear the 1 3 5 patterns in melodies and to write them.

MATERIALS : 1) Dictation slates and pennies
2) Piano

PROCEDURE : As the children are learning how to write out five number patterns, it's important to develop a feeling for the sound of the melodic triad 1, 3, 5. Help them to write out simple patterns on the staff.

1 3	1 3 5 3	1 3 5 3 5
1 3 5	1 3 5 3 1	1 3 1 3 5

Play these and other patterns for the children so they can learn the sound of the melodic triad. As before, play patterns on the piano and let the children tell you the numbers as a group. Since an objective of dictation is to hear groups of notes rather than just individual intervals, ask them to tell you if the triad notes were in the first or last part of the pattern. They could also tell you if it was ascending, 1 3 5 or descending, 5 3 1. When they're able to do this with ease, you can play patterns with the triad notes in the middle.

Play patterns on the piano for the children to write.

1234531	13531	12345311
1234535	1354321	1353123
123453	135313111	12313555

GAME 10—F   :   *WRITE MINE*

OBJECTIVE   :   The children play patterns for the class.

MATERIALS   :   1)   Staff slates and pennies
                          2)   Piano

PROCEDURE   :   If you enjoy letting the children get more involved, let them take turns writing out patterns on their slates and playing them for the other students to write. You may find that the children make their patterns more difficult than yours and might play them too fast. Help them to be good teachers too!

GAME 10–G :   *MORE NUMBERS*

OBJECTIVE :   To add high 6 7 8 and low $\overline{5}\ \overline{6}\ \overline{7}$ to the five note patterns and to introduce descending patterns.

MATERIALS :
1) Dictation slates and pennies
2) Number slates
3) Piano

PROCEDURE :   You can advance the difficulty of the melodic patterns as the children's abilities grow. Patterns that begin with a descending line such as D C B A G G are usually easy for the children to hear although they may need a little help writing it correctly.

Patterns using a full scale are important to use once the children become skilled at writing five-note patterns. If you play a pattern such as G A B C D E F G, they should be able to hear that the music continued to go up and write it correctly. Practice many patterns, increasing the difficulty only in small steps.

You can also familiarize the children with the low sounds $\overline{5}\ \overline{6}$ and $\overline{7}$ found below the 1 2 and 3.

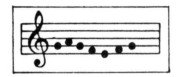

GAME 10–H :   *HEARD THIS BEFORE?*

OBJECTIVE :   To give children practice writing out short patterns from pieces they've already played (review pieces, not current ones). Then they can compare what they've written to the music.

MATERIALS :
1) Dictation slates and pennies
2) Music books
3) Piano

PROCEDURE :   The week before playing this game, ask everyone to bring their music books to class.

Explain that you're going to play beginnings, middles, or endings from pieces they've played before. They're to write down what you play on their staffs, think of the piece and look it up in their book to compare what they've written.

Always give them the starting note, since you'll be using notes other than G. Increase the difficulty as they become good at this. You can either ignore the concept of accidentals at this time, or include them.

GAME 10–I : *MAJOR OR MINOR*

OBJECTIVE : To familiarize the children with the difference between the major and minor triad sounds.

MATERIALS : 1) Number slates and pencils
2) Piano

PROCEDURE : *STEP ONE:* Before playing harmonic major and minor triads, you may want to let the children hear how they differ melodically. Give each of the children a dictation slate and ask them to write the numbers 1 2 3 4 5. Play this for them. You can play G A B C D if you like.

"I'm going to play these five notes, two times. The first time will be just as you heard it, but the second time I'm going to change one of the notes. I want you to draw a circle around the one that I changed."

Play 12345 (GABCD) and then play it minor (GAB♭ CD) lowering the third note one half-step. The children should circle the number 3 on their slates.

1 2 ③ 4 5

Repeat this several times, using different starting notes. Soon they'll realize that it's the third note that is altered each time. Explain that we call the first one a *major scale* and the second one a *minor scale*. Show them how you're playing the different scales on the piano.

Play several scales to see if they understand the difference between the major and minor sounds. Play major and minor 5-note scales for them to identify. Try this with major and minor triads as well. Always play two scales or two chords, one major and one minor in the same key, so they can compare the sounds. Be careful not to play the minor triad softer than the major one!

STEP TWO: Explain that a capital M can stand for major and a small m can stand for minor. Ask them to write one of each letter on their number slates. Explain that you'll play two chords. If the first one is major, they're to write a number 1 (for the first chord played) under the capital M. If the second chord is minor, they can write a 2 below the small m. Play both chords in the same key and same root note. Give several examples.

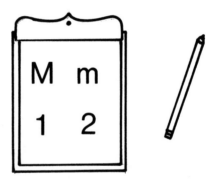

Once they can do this with ease you can try playing the same chord twice. If you played two F major chords, their slates should look like this:

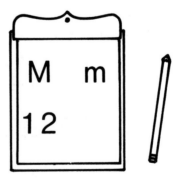

You can play more than two chords. If you played D major, D major and d minor, their slates would show:

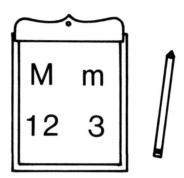

GAME 10—J : *THREE INTERVALS*

OBJECTIVE : To introduce the children to hearing different harmonic intervals.

MATERIALS : 1) Dictation slates and pennies
2) Piano

PROCEDURE : Ask the children to arrange the pennies as shown.

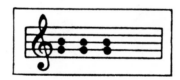

"What you've written sounds like this." Play three major harmonic thirds on the piano.

"I'm going to play that again. The bottom note will stay the same, but I'll change the top note. After I'm finished playing all three intervals, you can move the pennies."

Sample patterns to play:

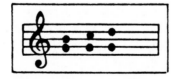

Perhaps you can think of other games to help children hear the different intervals.

GAME 10–K : *CHICKEN SOUP*

OBJECTIVE : To help children identify melodic patterns using simple rhythms. This game is good to play before children begin sight-reading as well as when they're being introduced to reading.

MATERIALS :
1) Song puzzle cards — 4 or more songs
2) Piano

PROCEDURE : Select four to seven cards from each of the songs so there are no duplications. Arrange the children in a semi-circle on the rug, facing away from the piano and toward the cards. Don't tell the children which color cards represent which songs.

"Will everyone sit cross-legged and put one hand on each knee, please? Good. You can see that each of these cards is one measure of music. I'm going to play one of these cards on the piano. When you find the card I'm playing, take your hands and quietly close them together. If I call on you, point out the card and turn it over. Any questions? OK, here's the first one."

Play the pattern only once unless they ask for it again. Be certain to pick one they'll be able to find easily or do several for practice so they get the idea of the game. Continue until all the cards are turned over.

Perhaps a little explanation is in order on why this game is called CHICKEN SOUP. The first time one of my theory classes played this game, I was cooking chicken soup upstairs for dinner that night. The aroma was inviting and something you couldn't miss. As I laid out the different colors of cards on the rug, someone said:

"Ymmmmmmmm. Those yellow cards look like chicken soup."

Then someone else decided the orange cards must be the carrots, the green cards the parsley and of course, the blue cards just had to be the cooking pot. We all had a good laugh and went on to fine the game most successful.

Next week when the class came back, everyone was asking to play CHICKEN SOUP. I looked a little bewildered.

"You know, the one with the chicken, parsley, carrots and the blue pot!"

GAME 10—L   :   *INTERVAL CIRCLE DICTATION*

OBJECTIVE   :   The game is played like 5—Q: INTERVAL CIRCLE but this time the children are to find the interval with their ears as well as their eyes.

MATERIALS   :   Alphabet cards — one set per student

PROCEDURE   :   Set up as described in the game INTERVAL CIRCLE page 94. (If by chance you don't have enough room, try modifying the set up.)

Give each child one set of alphabet cards and one blank card of the same color.

(optional)

Until the children become very skilled at hearing intervals, I suggest you play melodic intervals (play one note, then the second as opposed to the notes played at the same time). This is a little easier and gives the children more of a chance to succeed.

In the first several sessions keep the first note played the same throughout the game and change the second note. Tell the children the first note you play will be their first card.

SAMPLE GAME:

Play middle C on the piano.

"Hold your hand just above the C card."

Play D on the piano, one second above C.

"Move your hand to the note you think I'm playing. When I say GO, slap that card and call out the letter. . . . GO. Very good! You got it right. Let's try another one.

Play middle C.

"That's correct. Hands back above C card."

Play a C one octave higher. The students move their hands an octave up to the next C card.

"GO". They slap their cards and call out C.

You can use other intervals as well. It's suggested that you use around 3 intervals in this session and play each several times to reinforce their sound. Add more intervals in later sessions as the children are able. Later on you can have the lower note change during the session. Move carefully so the children continue to succeed at this.

180

GAME 10—M : *SONG PUZZLE SNAKES*

OBJECTIVE : Sight-reading is a skill that depends on the child's ability to relate notes to each other visually and not by note name alone. They need to be able to "hear" what the notes sound like before playing them. These song puzzle cards are short pieces that the children are very familiar with. They're able to look at the cards and "hear" the song's note patterns.

MATERIALS : Song puzzle cards

PROCEDURE : Explain the cards to the children. Point out that each card is one measure from the song. You're going to pass out the cards to them and they're going to try and arrange the cards in the right order for the song.

Explain that they're to turn their cards so that the dot is in the lower left-hand corner. If the card is turned upside down, it becomes a whole new note pattern. All the cards have a bar line on each side except for the first measure card, which has no line on the left side and the last card, which has a double bar to end the piece.

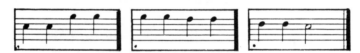

Place the title of the piece on the floor with the clef sign card underneath it. Pass out the cards.

Request that the children sing the song as they write it. Not only is this a valuable practice in sight-singing, but it helps them to keep their place.

If the children place a card out of sequence, let them discover this themselves. Once they finish, you can let them sing through the whole song using note names or numbers.

It's suggested that the children have some experience with sight-reading before these song puzzle cards are introduced. The song puzzle cards should be an easy, fun game, not a slow struggle to find the cards. This is important.

VARIATION: It's fun to have several song puzzle snakes being made at once. Give a few students a song and let them work independently as others write out other songs.

After they finish you can let them check each others snakes if you'd like.

Or, ask one group to close their eyes and switch around the cards. After they open their eyes, they can fix the cards.

Or, while their eyes are closed, turn over 6 − 7 cards. After they open their eyes, let them try to sing the card that's turned face down.

GAME 10—N : *SONG PUZZLE PASS OUT*

OBJECTIVE . To practice reading and playing a group of notes.

MATERIALS : Song puzzle cards

PROCEDURE : Pass out one to three cards to each student. Give them a chance to look at them and "sing the notes in their heads".

Asking for volunteers, let them take turns playing the cards on their instrument, one at a time. In the beginning they may need to read from their cards as they play the notes. As they're able, encourage them to look at the card, remember the starting note and play the notes on the card without looking.

A.M.

13

Name That Note

When you're reasonably sure that the students know the names of the notes in the treble clef and the bass clef, it's time to give them some real memory practice. The goal is to learn the notes so well that both clefs are easy to name.

The reason is unique to keyboard instruments—the sight-reader needs to read from both clefs at once. His eyes are continuously moving around both clefs. Although much of the reading will be relating one note to another through space relations rather than note name, if the child doesn't know one clef as well as the other, he'll be apt to stumble and make needless errors.

The games in this chapter give the children practice in thinking of both clefs at once. Since each clef is already memorized, these games are like dessert. Many are comfortable variations of games they've already played before. Some have exciting new twists. Almost all of the games can be played using not only bass clef or treble clef staff cards, but the clefless staff card as well. Or all three kinds at once.

GAMES FOUND IN THIS CHAPTER

GAME 11—A : *MATCH THIS CARD*

OBJECTIVE : To practice naming notes in both the treble and bass clef.

MATERIALS : 1) Staff cards
2) Alphabet cards

PROCEDURE : Play this game as described in previous chapters only use both treble and bass clef staff cards at once.

GAME 11—B : *MATCH THIS CARD—BACKWARDS*
GAME 11—C : *LINE 'EM UP*

OBJECTIVE : To practice naming notes in both the treble and bass clef.

MATERIALS : 1) Staff cards
2) Alphabet cards

PROCEDURE : Play these games as described in previous chapters only use both treble and bass clef staff cards at once.

GAME 11—D : *SHOW ME WITH NAMES*

OBJECTIVE . To practice naming notes in both the treble and bass clef.

MATERIALS : 1) Staff cards
2) Alphabet cards

PROCEDURE : Play this game as described in previous chapters only use both treble and bass clef staff cards at once.

GAME 11—E : *NAME IT*
GAME 11—F : *I CAN NAME IT*

OBJECTIVE : To practice naming notes in both the treble and bass clef.

MATERIALS : 1) Staff cards
2) Alphabet cards

PROCEDURE : Play these games as described in previous chapters only use both treble and bass clef staff cards at once.

GAME 11—G : *KEEP ON MATCHING*

OBJECTIVE : To practice naming both treble and bass clef notes at once.

MATERIALS : 1) Staff cards — treble and bass
2) Alphabet cards — one set

PROCEDURE .   Select seven staff cards from either clef, one of each of
the letters A, B, C, D, E, F, and G. Place them in a line.

Ask the children to place the alphabet cards
correctly under the staff cards.

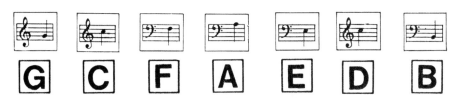

While they close their eyes, mix up the staff cards.

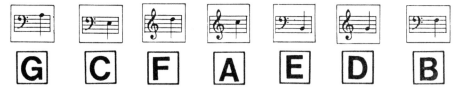

When they open their eyes, let them take turns moving
cards, one card at a time. They should place the cards
so that they're under the correct staff cards.

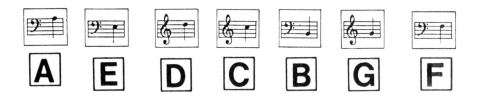

GAME 11–H :   *NAME THAT NOTE*

OBJECTIVE :   This is that favorite toss game with two clefs. Help the
students to answer correctly if they hesitate.

MATERIALS :
1) Two-staff board
2) Clefs
3) Toss note
4) Pencil or stick
5) Optional – gold coins or other play money

PROCEDURE :   Have the children place the clef signs on the staff board. Each child takes a turn standing at the bottom of the board to toss the note. After a child tosses, call out whether it landed on a line or space so there's no confusion. Let the child name the note.

Sometimes, it's fun to play this game with a little financial incentive. After the child names the note correctly, he can receive a gold coin. Several years ago, when a group of students was playing this game, the toss note kept landing in the treble clef, which I imagined they thought was easier for them to name.

I moved the pencil back farther, but the note still landed in the treble clef more often than the bass clef. Ah ha, I thought, an idea.

"Would you like to win gold coins for your correct answers?"

"Sure!"

"OK, you win one gold coin for a treble clef note and two gold coins for a bass clef note." It was simply remarkable how that toss note began landing in the bass clef!

GAME 11—I   :   *STAFF CARD PAIRS*

OBJECTIVE   :   To practice naming notes in both clefs.

MATERIALS   :   Staff cards

PROCEDURE   :   Divide the children into pairs. Give each pair of children four staff cards and hold on to the remaining ones. One child is to show the cards to his partner, one at a time, for him to name. When all four cards have been named, the children should return them to you in exchange for a new set of four cards. This time the other child names the notes. Each pair of children work at their own pace.

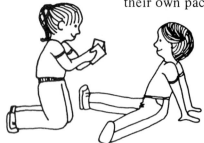

GAME 11–J : *STAFF CARD TEAMS*

OBJECTIVE : To practice identifying notes on both clefs.

MATERIALS : 1) Staff cards — both clefs
2) Alphabet cards — several sets for each team

PROCEDURE : Divide the children into three teams. Give each team a set of staff cards made up of several treble clef cards and several bass clef cards. Also give them the alphabet cards.

Each team is to line up the staff cards and place the correct alphabet cards underneath. As each team finishes they should check their cards.

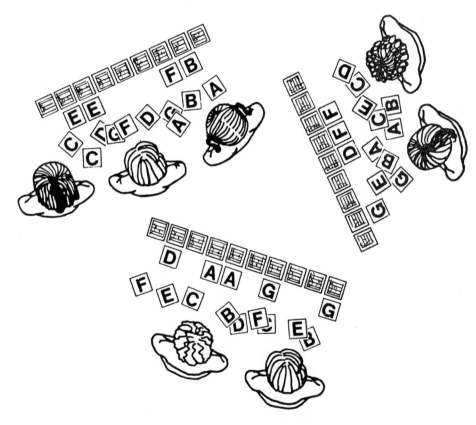

Each team can move around one position to check that set of cards. Once they've done that, they're to move the alphabet cards back into a pile, mix-up the staff cards, lay them out in a line again, and match the alphabet cards to the staff cards.

This can continue for several turns.

GAME 11–K :   *FISH*

OBJECTIVE   :   To play a "real-type" card game with the staff cards.

MATERIALS   :   1)   Staff cards – both clefs
2)   Alphabet cards – four sets of different colors than the staff cards. Check to see that you are using only the letters that will match evenly with the staff cards.

PROCEDURE   :   Explain the game to the children before passing out the cards. It proceeds like this.

Prepare by mixing up all the cards. Deal out four cards to every player. Place the remaining cards in a stack on the floor in the center of the circle of children. The object is to match up alphabet cards with staff cards by asking other players for the cards that match those in your hand.

Let's say Stan is dealt these cards:

Since he already has a pair, he places them face up on the floor in front of himself. He needs to find matching cards for those in his hand. It's his turn and he decides to try for a staff card D. He looks for someone who's holding mostly staff cards. He can tell this by the color of the cards. Staff cards are different colors than alphabet cards.

"Kathleen, do you have a staff card D?"

"Yes," and she gives him the staff card D that she's holding. The clef or octave doesn't matter.

"Thank you," and he places the pair of cards with the others. His turn is over.

If Kathleen hadn't had the card he asked for, she would have said, "no–go fish" and he would've taken a card from the center pile.

Each player only gets one turn whether they get the card they ask for or not. If a player uses up all his cards, he can draw one from the pile to stay in the game. The game ends when all the cards are paired up.

As with previous games, it isn't important who got the most sets.

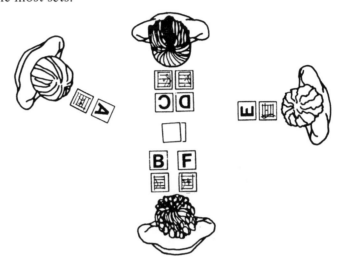

GAME 11–L : *OCTAVE PAIRS*

OBJECTIVE : To find all the octaves in both clefs.

MATERIALS : 1) Staff cards — both clefs
2) Alphabet cards — one set

PROCEDURE : Line the alphabet cards up in order. First, have the children line up the treble clef notes under the correct alphabet cards. Then, line up the bass clef staff cards.

The children may find it quite interesting if you let them discover that each note's stem ends an octave away, either up or down, depending on the stem.

GAME 11—M : *BINGO—BOTH CLEFS*

OBJECTIVE : When reading keyboard music, it's necessary to read back and forth between the bass clef and the treble clef and often both at once. This game gives the children practice thinking like that.

MATERIALS : 1) Bingo cards
2) Bingo discs
3) Alphabet cards — two sets

PROCEDURE : Let the children select a bingo card and four bingo discs. Place one alphabet card in front of them. Let's say it's a G. Each child is to check his card, looking for any G, either clef and any octave. Using the card below as an example, the child could have placed bingo discs over two notes in just one play. If a child doesn't see a note on his card, don't hassle him. He'll probably see it the next time that alphabet card appears.

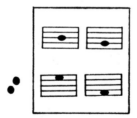

Continue placing alphabet cards down, one at a time, on top of each other, until all the bingo cards are full.

GAME 11—N : *NOT REALLY TRIADS*

OBJECTIVE : To review thirds and staff notes.

MATERIALS . Staff cards — both clefs (Throw in the clefless staff cards once they catch on to this game.)

PROCEDURE : Pass out all the staff cards to the children. This game is played like WIN A TRIAD, only staff cards are used instead of alphabet cards.

The game begins with one staff card on the rug in the middle of the players. Let's say that card is a **B** in the bass clef.

The third above B is D, so a child holding any D card, bass or treble, any octave, may put down his card. Let's say the quickest child put down D in the treble clef.

The next third is F, so any F can be played.

As in WIN A TRIAD, the player who put down the third card takes the first two cards and puts them in his hand with his others. The F becomes the new "root".

The game doesn't need a caller and the children will be able to play faster and easier if they place their staff cards on the floor and slide them into place.

This game is terribly exciting when the pink clefless staff cards are thrown in. The card can be a note in either clef (dot should go to the bottom), but once it's put down, it must stay that note for that round.

After someone wins the clefless staff card, it can be used for either clef again.

Position yourself above the cards (they'll be upside down to you) so you can push the cards to the children as they win them.

GAME 11—O : *SUPER SNAKE*

OBJECTIVE : To practice both clefs at once with all the excitement found in making snakes.

MATERIALS : 1) Alphabet cards — many sets
2) Staff cards — bass and treble (and clefless staff cards if you'd like)

PROCEDURE : This game is played just like STAFF CARD SNAKES, except treble and bass (and clefless) staff cards are used. You may need to toss in a few extra alphabet cards so it all works out evenly. The snake can be made either with thirds or in regular alphabet.

A variation of this would be to divide the students into three teams. Give one the treble clef and alphabet cards, the second, the bass clef and alphabet cards, and the third team the clefless staff cards and alphabet cards. After making their own snakes, they could move around and make a different one.

It's also fun if you rush over after their snake is made and admire it. After asking them to close their eyes, mix up some of the cards and let the students fix the snake.

A variation of this is to turn 7 - 10 cards face down. After opening their eyes, the students can take turns telling each other what the cards are.

GAME 11—P   :   *LEDGER LINE STAFF CARDS*

OBJECTIVE   :   To develop the children's ability to look at a ledger line note and name it without having to count up each line and space.

MATERIALS   :   1)   Ledger line staff cards
                          2)   Alphabet cards

PROCEDURE   :   Concentrate on a few cards at a time. You can play any of the games found in this chapter which use staff cards and alphabet cards. Help to develop the children's ability to look at the ledger line note and name it easily.

14

The Long
and The Short

Before my students do much sight-reading, I have them following along in the music book while a piece is being played. Often these pieces are considerably more difficult than ones they could play themselves.

They'll lay on the floor and move their finger over the music with great concentration, seemingly fascinated by the whole process.

One vital element in this musical comprehension is the ability to follow the rhythm of the piece. Without that, the music remains a mystery of curious looking shapes.

The games in this chapter use rhythm boards and cards. Each meter uses its own rhythm board of eight measures with the sizes of the note cards remaining the same. As you can see in the photos there is room for four quarter-notes in each measure of the $\frac{4}{4}$ board and only room for three on the $\frac{3}{4}$ board. Since the notes are sized in proportion to their duration the children can see clearly how they relate to each other.

NOTE: In the pictures in this chapter, the children are seated at the sides of the rhythm boards to accomodate the camera. Normally, they sit around the bottom of the boards.

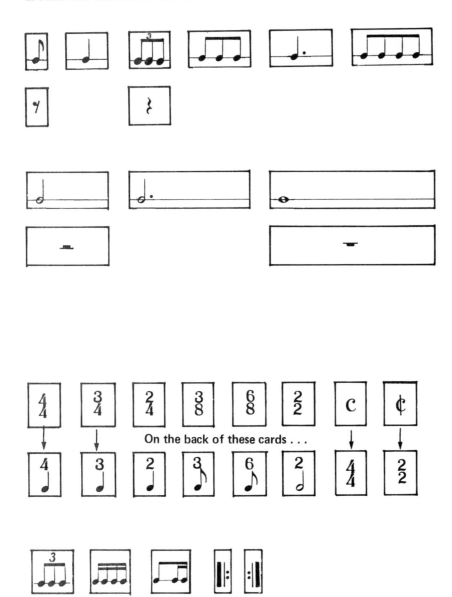

GAMES FOUND IN THIS CHAPTER

GAME 12–A : *REAL RHYTHMS*

OBJECTIVE : To introduce rhythms using "real looking" notes. The cards are made so each note and rest is of a length proportional to its value.

MATERIALS : 1) $\frac{4}{4}$ rhythm board
2) Rhythm cards

PROCEDURE : Place the rhythm board in front of the children and place the $\frac{4}{4}$ card in the small space in the upper left-hand corner. You can explain what this card means later in the session. Hold up a quarter-note card.

"Does anyone know what this is?"

"A blue."

"Right." Hold up a pair of eighth-notes card. "This?"

"That's a jello." Hold up a half-note card.

"Oh, a too."

Write out a rhythm using the cards in various combinations of blue, jello and toos for the children to clap. They're usually so curious about the different sizes of cards. In a session with six and seven-year-olds, they might be able to experiment with the different notes and rests for quite awhile. They can easily see how long the notes last because of the proportional length of the cards.

200

After they've clapped several rhythms and understand about the board, you can talk about the $\frac{4}{4}$ card. Turn it over so they can see the back.

front   back

"This is called a *time signature*. This one is $\frac{4}{4}$ (four four) time. It means that there are four quarter-notes in each of the measures." This can be illustrated easily by using four quarter-note cards.

GAME 12–B : *MAKING CHANGE*

OBJECTIVE : To teach the real names, quarter-notes, eighth-notes, half-notes, whole-notes and discuss their values within a measure.

MATERIALS : 1) Rhythm cards
2) $\frac{4}{4}$ rhythm board

PROCEDURE : Place the rhythm board in front of the children with the $\frac{4}{4}$ card in the corner. Place notes on the board as shown in the picture.

One way to explain this is to talk about the notes in terms of money. The whole-note is like a one dollar bill. The half-note, fifty cents. The quarter-notes are like twenty-five cents or a quarter. The length of the cards will make things clear. You can talk about how many counts each card receives in $\frac{4}{4}$ time.

When clapping whole-notes, you can call them "four" if the children want to continue using the words blue, jello and two for rhythms. Simply clap and say "four" at the same time and raise your hands up and down on the pulses as was done with "twos".

If you want to have some real money handy when you play this game, it'll probably help the children understand things even better.

GAME 12–C   :   *DOTTED RHYTHMS*

OBJECTIVE   :   To discuss dotted notes.

MATERIALS   :   1)   Rhythm cards
                 2) $\frac{4}{4}$ rhythm board

PROCEDURE   :   It'll be easy to understand the concept of a dotted note if you compare a dotted half-note with a regular half-note. Since children know that if a half-note is worth fifty cents, they'll be able to tell you that the dotted half-note would be worth seventy-five cents by looking at the cards. They'll see that a dot on the side of a note makes it longer. Discuss how much longer the note is.

When you feel that the children understand what the dot following a note means, discuss the dotted quarter-note using the cards. Practice clapping many rhythms using dotted notes.

GAME 12—D : *REST, REST, REST*

OBJECTIVE : To teach the children the names and values of the various kinds of rests (see rhythm card chart at beginning of chapter).

MATERIALS : 1) Rhythm cards
2) ⁴⁄₄ rhythm board

PROCEDURE : With the rhythm board in front of the children, explain that we often have rests in music. These are moments of silence that are important in making music expressive. Explain that each kind of note has its own kind of rest. Begin by showing them the quarter-rest. Let the children discover that it's the same size card as the quarter-note. Arrange one measure with a quarter-note, quarter-rest, quarter-note, quarter-rest. Point to the cards.

(clap . . .   rest . . .   clap . . .   rest)

"We count this measure one, two, three, four. We clap it like this—clap, (rest), clap, (rest)." You might want to whisper "rest" so it's easier to understand.
Write out several measures using combinations of quarter-notes and quarter-rests and let the children count and clap them. This shouldn't be difficult for them.

Half-rests and whole-rests will also interest the children. The children will discover how similar the two rests are if you turn the cards so that they look alike except for the length of the card. You may have your own way of telling the difference. One story goes like this:

"Suppose you lived over one-hundred years ago and your mother decided to invite President Abraham Lincoln to lunch. He knocked on your door and you let him in. He would probably be wearing his tall black hat. Since he has good manners, he would take his hat off when he came in, probably placing it on a table. We could pretend this line is the table and this is his hat sitting on top of it." Hold the half-note rest card up for the children.

"Well, everyone liked President Lincoln so much that your mother decided to ask him to come spend a week-end with your family. He arrives at the door and you're there to greet him. He's wearing his hat again and of course he takes it off as he steps inside. But since he's staying longer this time, a whole week-end, your mother places his hat in the closet, or like this whole-rest, under the table."

So the longer rest is under the line and the shorter rest is on top of the line. Hold up the cards and let the children tell you if they're right side up or not. (See photo at beginning of this chapter.)

Write out some rhythms using the whole- and half-rests. It's fun to be tricky and place the rest cards incorrectly to see if the children will catch it. Most likely you'll find that everyone pounces on the cards in an effort to turn them the right way. They think it's great fun and really stay alert.

GAME 12–E : *WRITE A SONG*

OBJECTIVE : This game gives the children practice writing out songs that they know on the rhythm board.

MATERIALS : 1) Rhythm cards
2) $\frac{4}{4}$ rhythm board

PROCEDURE :   *STEP ONE:* Select several songs written in $\frac{4}{4}$ time using only half-, quarter-, and pairs of eighth-notes that the children know well. As they become more advanced at this game, you can introduce other meters and other note values as well.

Sing the songs together, clapping and saying the words blue, jello, and too to the melody. Here are examples of two songs, *Lightly Row* and *Go Tell Aunt Rhody*.

LIGHTLY ROW

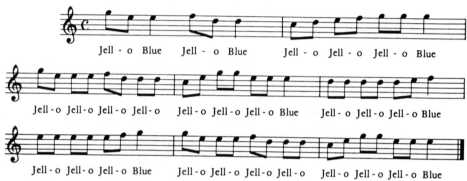

GO TELL AUNT RODY

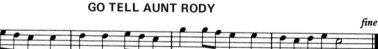

Let the children practice singing and clapping these songs in class and at home for several weeks. It'll take a little practice for them to be able to match the words with the songs.

STEP TWO: Write the songs out on the rhythm board using the cards. You can let the children take turns, writing one measure at a time. It's helpful to sing the song as it's being written.

GAME 12—F : *WHAT SONG IS THIS?*

OBJECTIVE : This game develops the children's ability to look at a rhythm and "hear" how it sounds. Play this game only with songs that the children have already practiced writing out themselves.

MATERIALS : 1) Rhythm cards
2) $\frac{4}{4}$ rhythm board

PROCEDURE : Place the $\frac{4}{4}$ card in the upper left-hand corner of the $\frac{4}{4}$ board. Without telling the children which songs you've selected, write it out using the rhythm cards. Can you tell which song the children are studying?

Position yourself away from the children. Once they figure out the title of the song you've written, they can come over to you and whisper the title in your ear. Often a child will forget the title, yet know what the song sounds like. As long as they can sing a little of the melody, that counts.

With practice the children will be able to figure out songs without clapping them, but when you first play this game, it's a good idea to clap the rhythm together.

Or they may clap it "silently" with one finger on their cheek so as to not distrub anyone else.

Finish by clapping and singing the song together. It's okay if everyone isn't always able to guess a song. It doesn't help for them to feel hassled. Just smile reassuringly and continue, perhaps writing out another song, or moving on to another game.

GAME 12–G : *GUESS MY SONG*

OBJECTIVE : The children write out rhythms of songs.

MATERIALS :
1) Paper and pencils
2) Rhythms cards
3) $\frac{4}{4}$ rhythm board

PROCEDURE : Ask the children to write out the rhythms of some songs on paper at home. Perhaps, they could choose one or two songs from a list you give them. Explain that they're not to look in the book or have mother help. This will help you know how well they're understanding the lessons. Show them how to write rhythms on paper.

When they come the next week, look over their papers to see if you can guess the songs they chose. Let them take turns writing out their songs for the other children to guess, without using their papers.

The child should be the one to step away from the group. The other children are to figure out what song was written and one at a time, go over to the child and whisper the title in his ear.

GAME 12–H :   *TEACHING $\frac{3}{4}$ TIME*

OBJECTIVE :   To introduce the children to $\frac{3}{4}$ time.

MATERIALS :   1)   Rhythm cards
                 2) $\frac{3}{4}$ rhythm board

PROCEDURE :   The children will notice that the $\frac{3}{4}$ board is smaller than the $\frac{4}{4}$ as well as a different color. The children may be able to figure out that the $\frac{3}{4}$ card means that there will be three beats in each measure and a quarter-note gets one of those beats. Let the children experiment with the board and various rhythm cards. They'll soon see that the whole-note doesn't belong in $\frac{3}{4}$ time.

                You can play many of the games found in this chapter which deal with the $\frac{4}{4}$ board.

GAME 12—I : *RHYTHM CARD SNAKES*

OBJECTIVE : The rhythm boards and cards help the children understand the division of beats and how they're divided into even measures. This game is designed to reinforce what they've learned and to help them become more independent in their thinking of rhythm.

MATERIALS : 1) Rhythm cards
2) Blue sticks — for bar lines

PROCEDURE : Seat the children in a semi-circle in front of you. Place the $\frac{4}{4}$ card facing them and to your right.

"I'd like to write a $\frac{4}{4}$ rhythm snake. Since we won't be using the rhythm board, the blue sticks from blue jello can be our bar lines." Write a few sample measures for them, like the one shown below:

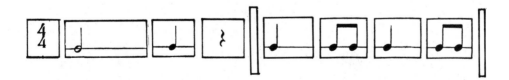

Give one blue stick to each child. "I'm going to write more measures. Do you think you can take turns putting in the bar lines?" Write more measures, letting them tell you where the bar lines should go.

GAME 12–J : *RHYTHM MIX-UP*

OBJECTIVE : To reinforce the concept of dividing rhythms into measures and introduce the concept of the tie as it relates to rhythm.

MATERIALS : 1) Rhythm cards
2) Blue sticks

PROCEDURE : Ask everyone to close their eyes. Write out a rhythm with the cards without any bar lines.

Ask the children to open their eyes. "Can you tell me where the bar lines should go?" Holding one blue stick, glide it just above the cards and let the children tell you to "STOP" when they think a bar line is needed. Be sure to make the first rhythms easy and obvious.

210

Ask the children to close their eyes. As you re-arrange the cards, switch the meter card to $\frac{3}{4}$ or $\frac{2}{4}$. After the children open their eyes, let them put in the bar lines as before. Some watchful student or two will certainly spot the switched meter card and encourage everyone to divide the rhythm accordingly.

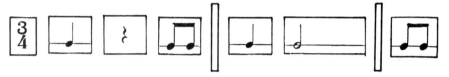

When the children want to put a bar line right down the middle of the half-note card, you can talk about the concept of using a tie. They'll find this most intriguing.

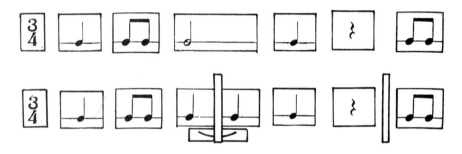

GAME 12—K   :   *RHYTHM SONG SNAKES*

OBJECTIVE   :   To write out familiar melodies in snake form rather than on the rhythm boards.

MATERIALS   :   1) Rhythm cards
                  2) Blue sticks

PROCEDURE   :   Place the rhythm cards and blue sticks out for the children. Select a song they all know and let them write it out, each child taking a measure. Watch to see if the child who writes the last measure remembers to put in a double bar line. Let the children make the snake by themselves once you are confident that they understand how to do it.

211

GAME 12-L : *KNEE SLAPPERS*

OBJECTIVE : To teach the children to distinguish between pulse and rhythm. Often students are good at imitating rhythms, but may benefit from fitting these rhythms into an even pulse.

MATERIALS : Two hands and a good brain

PROCEDURE : Seat the children in a semi-circle and ask them to sit cross-legged. With your right hand on your right knee, tap out the rhythm of a simple song they're very familiar with. *Twinkle, Twinkle, Little Star* is a good example. The children will think it's fun if you tap out other rhythms of songs for them to guess.

"Everyone raise your right hand high in the air. Good. Tap out *Twinkle* together. One, two, ready, go." Everyone taps out *Twinkle* with their right hands on their right knees. It's good if everyone sings along as they tap.

"OK—that was good. Now, watch this." As you sing *Twinkle*, tap out the pulse with your left hand on your left knee. After showing them once, let them do it by themselves.

Next, you can let half the class tap the pulse with their left hands on their left knee and the other half of the class tap the rhythm of *Twinkle* with their right hands.

"You did that really well. Watch the next step." As you tap out the pulse with your left hand, tap out the rhythm of *Twinkle* with your right hand at the same time. The children should be eager to try it themselves.

It'll be less confusing if you don't tap along with them, since you're sitting facing them. They'll also think better on their own and not just follow you.

Ask everyone to do this at home after you've watched their mothers try it with the children.

In later sessions, try more advanced songs as the children are able to do *Twinkle* easily. The children will enjoy taking turns, each doing one phrase.

GAME 12–M :   *TEACHING OTHER METERS*

OBJECTIVE   :   To introduce $\frac{2}{4}$, $\frac{6}{8}$, $\frac{3}{8}$, $\frac{2}{2}$ time. By this time the children should feel comfortable clapping the rhythms without always needing to sing along with the "blue and jello" words.

MATERIALS :   1)   Rhythm cards
2)   Rhythm boards

PROCEDURE :   As the children become comfortable with rhythms in $\frac{3}{4}$ and $\frac{4}{4}$ time, you can introduce the other meters. The children will be curious about the different boards and if given time, will be able to figure out the time signatures they represent. Just lay out plenty of rhythm cards and the possible choices in time signature cards. They'll discover which notes fit and which don't fit with the various meters.

Write rhythms with the boards as well as songs.

A fun game might be to divide the children into teams and give each one a different rhythm board. After each team has written either a song or a rhythm, they can take turns clapping each others creations.

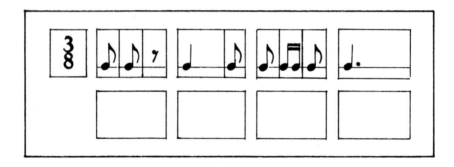

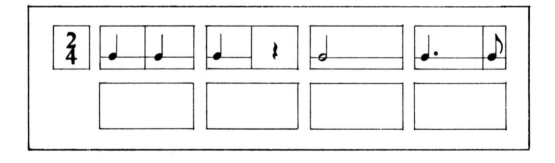

GAME 12—N :   *DUPLE, TRIPLE OR QUADRUPLE*

OBJECTIVE :   To give the children a feel for the different meters as they listen to music.

MATERIALS :   Piano or another instrument

PROCEDURE :   With the children, clap various meters, emphasizing the strong and weak pulses. Talk about which meters are called duple, which are triple and which are quadruple. They're all simple meters. As the children's musical education progresses, you could discuss compound meters.

DUPLE METER	$\frac{2}{2}$	$\frac{2}{4}$	$\frac{2}{8}$
TRIPLE METER	$\frac{3}{2}$	$\frac{3}{4}$	$\frac{3}{8}$
QUADRUPLE METER	$\frac{4}{2}$	$\frac{4}{4}$	$\frac{4}{8}$
COMPOUND DUPLE	$\frac{6}{2}$	$\frac{6}{4}$	$\frac{6}{8}$
COMPOUND TRIPLE		$\frac{9}{4}$	$\frac{9}{8}$
COMPOUND QUADRUPLE	$\frac{12}{4}$	$\frac{12}{8}$	$\frac{12}{16}$
QUINTUPLE METER	$\frac{5}{4}$		

At this time, it's probably necessary to discuss only those they've learned or are finding in their music. They'll find it easy to understand if you play some simple songs and let them clap along with you, seeing if they can say 1 2 3 or 1 2 3 4 or 1 2 as you play. Emphasize the pulse as you play.

GAME 12—O : *NOTES AND RESTS*

OBJECTIVE : To teach students about the different values of notes and rests and their relationship to each other and how they fit into the various time signatures. The design of the game challenges students to "mathematically" relate these concepts without the interaction of melody or harmony.

MATERIALS :
1) N and R game board (22" x 28") blue
2) Two sets N and R cards — one green, one yellow
3) Walking Woodstock (Peanuts character). You can use any figure you like. They are nearly 3" high, plastic, wind-up and walking. Found in department, toy and children's stores.

USES :
1) To familiarize young students with the various shapes of notes and rests
2) To learn the names of the notes and rests
3) To learn their time value in relation to time signatures
4) To understand how notes and rests fit into measures
5) To clap rhythms
6) To take rhythmic dictation
7) To inspire students, teachers and parents to use the board and cards to create their own games for learning.

Special thanks and appreciation to Penny Kunkel and Evy Olson for showing me a rhythm game they created and used with their students in Lincoln, Nebraska which began my thinking about Notes and Rests.

Pattern available from Music 19

15

Snakes and People On the Piano

At this point, your students will thoroughly know the names of the notes on the staff, be able to clap out rhythms using many combinations of notes and rests, be able to write down simple melodies on a staff after one or two hearings, and identify the various musical signs. One step is left before the children can begin actual reading—relating what they know to their instrument.

Since all musicians need to be comfortable with the keyboard, not just the pianists should play these games. Perhaps, you've already taught your students the names of the keys. If so, these games will help them relate octaves and where each note is found.

You may find it necessary to play only games 13–A through 13–C before attempting sight-reading from regular music books. Games 13–D through 13–J are optional and can be used to teach groups and to reinforce what 13–C teaches.

Games 13–K through 13–L are for string students and should be preceeded with study of 13–A through 13–D.

GAMES FOUND IN THIS CHAPTER

GAME 13—A :   *THREE FINGERS—TWO FINGERS*

OBJECTIVE :   To teach the black note patterns and what "up and down the keyboard" means.

MATERIALS :   1)   Piano — step one
2)   Piano and alphabet people — step two

PROCEDURE :   *STEP ONE:* Ask everyone to hold up three fingers (2 3 & 4) with their right hands and two fingers with their left hands.

"Very good. OK, put your hands in your laps. Now, up again with those fingers. Good. Down . . . Up . . . Down . . . Up. I told you this would be easy!" and everyone will laugh.

"Keep your fingers in the air. I want you to line up at the piano, shoulder to shoulder and silently place your fingers on the black notes. Stand close to each other so that all the black notes are covered."

Ask the person at the lower end of the keyboard to play his two black notes and then his three black notes, one note at a time. It'll help to demonstrate this for them first. Continue up the keyboard letting each child play his notes in turn.

"We call this going *up* the keyboard. Now let's try going *down*." Let each child play his notes, one at a time.

The children will think it's great fun to play up and down the keyboard this way and will find the sound of the pentatonic scale pleasant.

STEP TWO: In the children's private lessons, you can teach the names of the individual notes on the keyboard if they haven't already learned them.

First, review the pattern of the black notes. Because of the songs they've learned, my students are very comfortable positioning the r.h. in a 5-note scale on C (one octave above middle C). I teach this key first. Carefully, we discuss how the black notes can help us find other C's and move a C alphabet person up and down the keyboard, finding all the C's.

At the child's pace, we learn the names of all the white keys.

GAME 13—B : *PEOPLE ON THE PIANO*

OBJECTIVE : To give the children practice recognizing the names of the keys on the piano.

MATERIALS : 1) Alphabet people
2) Piano

PROCEDURE : Pass out all the people to the children and ask them to place them on the correct keys of the piano. They may place the people anywhere on the keyboard.

Have them close their eyes. Switch the people around so some are incorrect. The children can open their eyes, step back up to the piano and take turns finding a person in the wrong spot and placing him on the right key.

The sight of these cute people on the keys makes this a most inviting game.

GAME 13—C : *THIS NOTE AND THAT KEY*

OBJECTIVE : To introduce the children to matching each staff note to one key on the piano.

MATERIALS :
1) Alphabet people
2) One dictation slate
3) Penny

PROCEDURE : Once the children have learned the names of the keys on the piano, you can begin relating them to the staff. Place the dictation slate on the music stand of the piano. You can begin by showing the children where the line notes of the treble clef are found. Hold the penny on middle C on the staff and place the alphabet person C on the piano C. Do this with all the line notes.

Be certain to see that the children relate high notes on the piano to high notes on the staff, paying careful attention to the octave notes.

The children will enjoy seeing if they can find the right note on the piano, if you move the penny on the staff. They'll also think it's fun if you give them the penny, point to a note on the piano and let them place the penny on the staff. You can leave the alphabet people on the piano for as long as they need the reference.

At a later time, you can relate the bass clef note to the piano in the same fashion.

From these games with the dictation slate, penny and alphabet people, the children should be able to know where all the notes on the staff are found on the keyboard. You can move to setting "real" music books on the piano and letting them find the notes on the piano. From there, it's a simple step to beginning sight-reading.

Perhaps, you'd like to play more games with this subject. If so, the following eight games were developed to do this. The children like them a lot.

GAME 13–D : *NATURAL HALF STEPS BC AND EF*

OBJECTIVE : To point out the natural half-steps BC and EF.

MATERIALS : 1) Alphabet people
  2) Piano

PROCEDURE : Play this game when the children really know the names of the notes on the keyboard. With the children, discover which two pairs of white notes do not have a black note between them. B–C and E–F. Since a half-step occurs "naturally" between them, we can call them *natural half-steps*. Play PEOPLE ON THE PIANO, concentrating only on the EF and BC notes.

GAME 13—E :   *LINE UP A KEYBOARD*

OBJECTIVE :   If you're teaching one child at a time, you may not find it necessary to play some of these games exactly as they're described. Most likely, you can relate the staff to the keyboard effectively with the child seated at the piano. However, if you have a group of wiggling children, it can get rather crowded around one keyboard. The objective of this and the following games is to *teach where each note on the staff is located on the keyboard.* With this game, we set up our "keyboard" on the floor.

MATERIALS :   1)   Alphabet cards — four sets, four colors
2)   Blue jello sticks — the long length stick only

PROCEDURE :   Give four children the four sets of alphabet cards and ask them to line them up as shown.

C D E F G A B C D E F G A B C D E F G A B C D E F G A B

Remove the lower cards C D. This leaves those notes, treble and bass clef notes, that we've been studying. Explain that the alphabet cards represent the keys on the piano, each octave being a different color.

The blue sticks can be placed with the cards to represent the black keys on the piano. The children should be able to tell you where to put the sticks by following the natural half-step patterns. Afterwards, point out the pattern of two sticks, three sticks, two sticks, etc., which are just like the black keys on the piano.

"Close your eyes." Move the sticks around to the wrong places. "Open your eyes."

"Oh. We heard you moving those sticks around. But we can fix them really fast."

Since the "keyboard" is long enough, each child will have several sticks in front of himself to fix. The "keyboard" can be checked by looking for the natural half-steps.

GAME 13—F : *STAFF AND "KEYBOARD"*

OBJECTIVE : To relate the staff notes to the "keyboard".

MATERIALS : 1) Alphabet cards — four sets, four colors
2) Blue jello sticks — long length only
3) Two-staff board
4) Clefs
5) Toss note
6) Alphabet people

PROCEDURE : Line up your "keyboard" with the alphabet cards and blue jello sticks, placing the staff board above it and the alphabet people, in order, to one side.

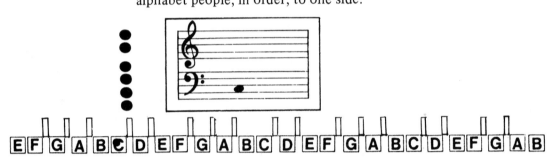

Placing the toss note on one note on the staff and then pointing to the "keyboard" note, show the children how one note on the staff matches one note on the "keyboard". It's helpful to relate this to the piano keyboard as well.

Let the children take turns matching staff notes to the "keyboard" by placing the matching letter alphabet person on the correct alphabet card.

GAME 13—G : *KEYBOARD RELAY*

OBJECTIVE : To have some fun relating the keyboard to the staff.

MATERIALS : 1) One- and two-staff board — use face down
2) Dictation slates — two
3) Pennies — two
4) Alphabet people

224

5) Staff cards
6) Alphabet cards
7) Blue jello sticks — use long length only

PROCEDURE :   Set up the materials as shown. Divide the children into two teams and ask one mother to join each team.

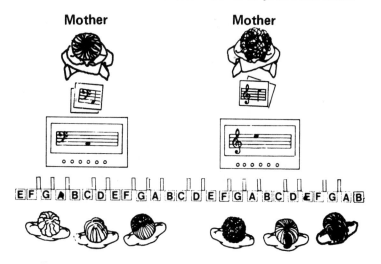

The sequence for each team is:

1. Mother turns over one staff card.
2. One child places the penny on the dictation slate to match the staff card note.
3. The child selects the alphabet person with the letter that matches the note.
4. The child touches the alphabet person to the correct note on the "keyboard" for the mother to see.
5. Child returns alphabet person to proper place in line.

In another session, you can include the real keyboard. After the child touches the alphabet person to the "keyboard" note, he can go to the keyboard and touch the right key. You can ask two mothers to stand at the piano to check out each teams' notes.

It's good to section off the portion of the keyboard that you're relating to the staff. Slide an alphabet card between the keys to the left of low E (bass clef) and another card to the right of high A (treble clef).

The children will see that the treble clef notes we've learned fit into less than two octaves, and the same for the bass clef.

GAME 13—H : *HIGH AND LOW*

OBJECTIVE : To impress upon the child that each key on the piano is found in only one place on the staff.

MATERIALS : 1) Alphabet people
2) Staff cards — use one clef at a time
3) Piano

PROCEDURE : While standing at the piano, place the middle C and the high A (treble clef) staff cards on the music stand. Place them over their respective notes.

Let someone place the two matching alphabet people on the right keys. Leave these two people and their cards in place during this game.

Place two cards, say G and G between the C and A. Talk about which G is high and which is low. Let the children place the two alphabet people on the piano.

Do this with the other octaves.

GAME 13—I : *PLACE THE PEOPLE*

OBJECTIVE : To practice finding individual notes on the keyboard.

MATERIALS : 1) Alphabet people
2) Staff cards — use one clef at a time at first
3) Piano

PROCEDURE : Place the alphabet people on the floor and give each child a staff card. They're to decide the name of the note on their card and find the matching alphabet person. Once the child has selected his alphabet person, he can come up to the piano. One at a time the child places his staff card on the music stand and the alphabet person on the correct key.

Once his person is correct, he can trade in his staff card for a new one and return to the alphabet people to find the right person. The game continues until everyone has had several turns.

GAME 13—J : *TOSS, NAME, AND FIND IT*

OBJECTIVE : To practice relating the staff to the keyboard.

MATERIALS : 1) Two-staff board
2) Toss note
3) Clefs
4) Alphabet people
5) Piano

PROCEDURE : Place the two-staff board on the floor and let the children place the clef signs on it. The game is just like NAME THAT NOTE and includes finding the note on the keyboard.

Sequence:
1. Child tosses note.
2. Names note.
3. Selects matching alphabet person.
4. Places alphabet person on matching piano key.

GAME 13–K : *STAFF CARDS AND THE "KEYBOARD"*

OBJECTIVE : This game is for relating the staff cards to the "keyboard".

MATERIALS :
1) Alphabet cards — four sets, four colors
2) Blue jello sticks — use long length only
3) Staff cards

PROCEDURE : Line up the "keyboard" using the blue jello sticks and the alphabet cards. Let the children place the correct staff card under the matching alphabet card.

When they've done this successfully, ask them to close their eyes. Mix up the staff cards and also the black note sticks. When they open their eyes, they can fix things back up. Switch the children around so each one has the opportunity to work with both clefs.

GAME 13–L : *I'M A STRING PLAYER*

OBJECTIVE : To help students studying a string instrument to relate the staff to their instruments. They'll lay out an "alphabet card" fingerboard on the floor. At a later time, this approach will help them to understand scales.

MATERIALS : 1) The children's instruments
2) Alphabet cards — four sets, four colors

PROCEDURE : String students have an advantage over piano students, in that their instruments are portable and there are fewer notes to learn. Most likely you'll want to familiarize your students with the names of the keys on the piano and how they relate to the staff, but your main emphasis will, of course, be with their own instruments.

Review the names of the open strings. Lay out these cards using four different colors. The violin is used as an example.

Violin

If the children have played the game NATURAL HALF-STEPS BC AND EF, they'll be able to lay the rest of the notes by following the natural half-steps. Do one string at a time, going up in order. They can place the natural half-step cards close together and leave a space between the others.

Violin

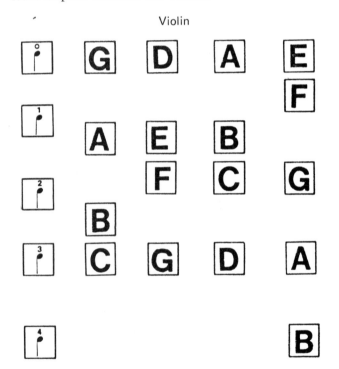

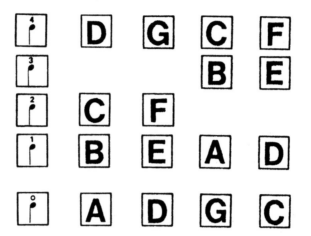

Since duplicating the open string notes may be confusing, they can be left out of this initial presentation. Including the finger number orange cards along one side of the "fingerboard" may be helpful.

Find these notes on the violin and allow the children to feel that their fingers are close together for the natural half-step notes.

Using a staff board, notes and alphabet people, show the children where the notes on their instrument are found on the staff.

After this initial explanation, the previous games 13—F through 13—K can be adapted and used with the floor "fingerboard".

GAME 13—M :   *FIND THIS NOTE*

OBJECTIVE   :   To practice relating notes on the violin, viola and cello to the staff.

MATERIALS   :   1)   Child's instrument
2)   Dictation slates and pennies

PROCEDURE   :   Practice this game as a group before playing it as described.

Divide the children into pairs, giving each one a dictation slate, penny and an instrument. One child places the penny on the staff and the other child finds the note on his instrument. The children can take turns.

A.M.

16
Scales and Key Signatures

One of the most difficult concepts for students to understand, is often the system of key signatures and scales. It's hoped that you'll find this approach to simplify the study of the circle of fifths and how the scales are formed. By following these ideas, students can be writing out major scales with sharps in one class period, and major scales with flats not long after. Once they understand the concept, each child is ready to study the scales on their instrument. They'll be able to concentrate on the correct techniques, since they'll understand how scales are formed and be comfortable with the system.

233

GAME 14—A : *MAJOR SCALES—SHARPS*

OBJECTIVE : To introduce the children to scales and keys. To teach the scales C Major, G Major, D Major, A Major, and B Major.

MATERIALS :
1) Alphabet cards — two sets, two colors
2) Blank card — same color as one set a.c.
3) Pink sharp/flat cards — use sharp side
4) Alphabet person — one
5) Piano and bench

PROCEDURE : The concept of scales and keys is introduced at the piano using the ear, rather than the half-step, whole-step pattern, to arrange the sharps. This game can be done individually or in a small group after the children have been playing their instruments for some time. They should be very familiar with the sound of a major scale. Learning scales this way should be easy for them. Some of the information is simply given to them, other things they're able to discover on their own.

Listed are the suggested steps.

STEP ONE: Play a C major scale on the piano, one octave up and down. On the piano bench in front of the children are the cards. Explain that a scale consists of eight notes. This first scale is CDEFGAB, with the blank card being C.

235

"You can see that I used only the white notes on the piano and no sharps. I'd like to play a scale with one sharp. To find this scale, I move five notes up on the piano, up a fifth to G. Can someone arrange our cards to spell a G scale?"

STEP TWO: Ask the children to see if they can tell you which note needs the sharp. Play the G scale, one octave up and down, using only the white notes. It should be easy for them to hear that the F needs a sharp. Place a sharp card above the F card in your scale.

Place an F card next to a sharp card on the music stand of the piano. "We can keep track of the sharps here."

STEP THREE: "I'd like to find the scale using two sharps. We can go up a fifth again, to D." Have one child arrange the cards so that they read DEFGABC blank card. Place the sharp card over F. "We keep the old sharp and add one new one."

Play the D scale using only the F sharp, letting the children tell you the new sharp. They'll hear that C needs the sharp. Place a sharp over C.

Place a C next to the F on the music stand.

STEP FOUR: "Our new sharp was which degree of the scale? Right, C is the seventh degree in the D scale. Next is our scale with three sharps. Anyone think that new third sharp will also be the seventh degree in the new scale? Let's watch for it."

STEP FIVE: "A scale with three sharps. Up a fifth to . . . right, A. Can someone arrange the cards?" Instruct the child to arrange the alphabet cards in the correct order first. Second, he can place the sharps on in order—F, then C. This procedure is important.

Play the scale on A with only F sharp and C sharp, letting the children hear the new sharp. They might pounce on the G sharp as soon as they hear the incorrect G natural played. Place a sharp card over the G card.

Place a G next to F and C on the music stand.

STEP SIX: "Ah ha—the new sharp was the seventh degree again. Do you think we've found a pattern? Perhaps the scale with four sharps will also add the sharp on the seventh degree as well. The scale with four sharps will begin on . . . E. (Arrange the alphabet cards.) Before putting on the sharps, let's put an alphabet person on D, the seventh degree and predict the new sharp." Then add the sharps in order, F C G.

STEP SEVEN: The children should have no trouble hearing that the new sharp is indeed D, the seventh degree, and no doubt someone will place the sharp card over D.

Add D to the sharps on the music stand.

STEP EIGHT: Ask someone to arrange the cards in the scale for five sharps, B major. Place the alphabet person on the seventh degree, A, first. Then add the sharps in order, F C G D.

STEP NINE: Play the B scale, using the four sharps F C G and D, letting the students hear that A is the new sharp.

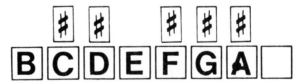

Place the A card on the music stand.

This is as far as is suggested to go with the sharp scales at this time. In later study, the students can learn

238

F# and C# major scales. In this early study, it's less confusing if they learn to think of F as *one flat* and C as *no sharps* or *flats*. Also, these are the keys they'll be using the most in their playing and sight-reading.

In another session, repeat the procedure, going through all the scales at the piano. This will help them understand the steps of forming scales. It's quite helpful to ask them to play the scales at home and in lessons. Even non-piano students will benefit from playing scales on the piano.

GAME 14–B :   *F C G D A*

OBJECTIVE   :   To memorize the order of sharps used in scales. (Hopefully this is more enlightening than memorizing "fat cats go down and eat breakfast"!)

MATERIALS :   None

PROCEDURE :   Seat the children before you and explain that you'd like to play "follow the leader" to learn the sharps. These are suggested steps. Adapt them, if necessary, to fit your own style of teaching.

Do each step by yourself. Pause and let the children imitate you. Keep the pulse steady and the rhythm even.

STEP ONE: Hit the floor 4 times with your hands. One strong pulse and 3 weak pulses.

hands x x x x

Pause for them to imitate.

STEP TWO: Do step one and add slapping your knees 4 times.

slapping:

hands   slapping

Pause for them to imitate you.

STEP THREE: Do step one and step two and add clapping.

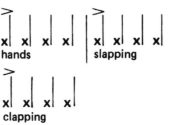

hands   slapping

clapping

Pause for them to imitate you.

STEP FOUR: Do steps one, two, three, in a row and add touching your shoulders.

hands   slapping

clapping   touching

Pause for them to imitate you.

STEP FIVE: Do steps one, two, three, four in a row and add tapping the top of your head.

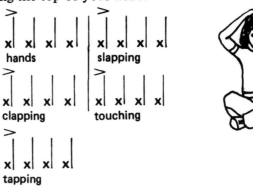

hands   slapping

clapping   touching

tapping

Pause for them to imitate you.

240

STEP SIX: Go through the whole sequence with motions. Say the letters on the strong pulses. Add one letter at a time, pausing each time for them to imitate you.

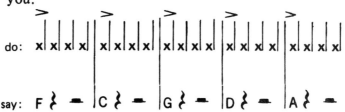

STEP SEVEN: Say F C G D A with the motions and only one beat.

do: x| x| x| x| x|

say: F·   C   G   D   A

Pause for them to imitate you.

The children will begin to memorize the order of sharps after this routine and have a good time doing it. This game is really easy to play, but hard to write out!

GAME 14–C :	*WRITE A SCALE–SHARPS*
OBJECTIVE :	The children practice writing scales themselves.
MATERIALS :	1) Alphabet cards
	2) Blank cards
	3) Alphabet people
	4) Pink sharp/flat cards — use sharp side
PROCEDURE :	Give each child:
	1 set of alphabet cards and matching blank card
	1 alphabet person
	5 pink sharp/flat cards

Review the previous game, F C G D A, to refresh their memories on the order of sharps.

Go through each scale together. Do C first, then G, D, A, E, and B. The steps for each scale would be:

STEP ONE: Arrange alphabet cards and blank card. The example is E.

STEP TWO: Place the alphabet person on the 7th degree. This is a reminder that this will be the last sharp added.

STEP THREE: Add sharps, in order, until one is placed over the letter with the alphabet person.

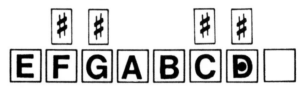

Practice writing each of the scales. If the students practice this at home as well as in class, they should be able to memorize the sharp scales over the course of several weeks.

GAME 14–D : *FIX THE SHARPS*

OBJECTIVE : To practice naming key signatures.

MATERIALS :
1) Alphabet cards — one set
2) Pink sharp/flat cards

PROCEDURE : Lay out the cards as shown, while the students close their eyes.

The alphabet card represents the *name* of the key, and the sharp card, the *number* of sharps in that key. Let the children take turns moving only one sharp card at a time until everything is fixed. Repeat several times.

GAME 14—E : *KEY SIGNATURES-SHARPS*

OBJECTIVE : To learn how key signatures are written on the staff.

MATERIALS :
1) Alphabet cards
2) Blank cards
3) Alphabet people
4) Pink sharp/flat cards — use sharp side
5) Dictation slates
6) Mini sharps
7) One-staff board
8) Clef
9) Felt sharps for one-staff board

PROCEDURE : Give one dictation slate and five mini-sharps to each child. Position the one-staff board with clef in view of the children.

Have the children write out the scales, in order, as you did in the previous game, WRITE A SCALE-SHARPS. After writing each scale, let them arrange the key signatures on their dictation slates, using the mini-sharps. They'll be able to place the sharps correctly if you also place each key signature on the one-staff board.

A.M.

243

GAME 14—F :   *I KNOW MY KEY SIGNATURES*

OBJECTIVE .   To be able to look at the pattern of sharps on the staff and identify the key signature easily.

MATERIALS :   1)   One-staff board
2)   Clef
3)   Felt sharps

PROCEDURE :   By this time the students should know the order of sharps (F C G D A) and know how many sharps each key contains.

Place the staff board on the floor in front of them and let them place the clef correctly. Review the key signatures by going over each key using the materials.

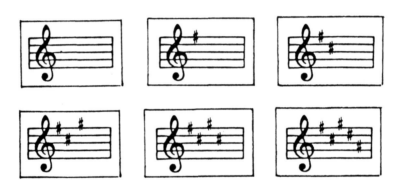

STEP ONE: Ask the children to close their eyes and rearrange one of the sharps a little.

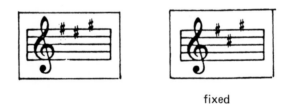

fixed

After they open their eyes, call on one of them to fix it. As they're able, rearrange more than one sharp for them to fix.

STEP TWO: While the children close their eyes, rearrange the sharps. After they open their eyes, call out a key.

244

They're to fix the sharps on the staff and possibly take away or add sharps.

A   corrected

GAME 14—G : *KEY SIGNATURE PAIRS*

OBJECTIVE : To practice writing the key signatures.

MATERIALS : 1) Alphabet cards
2) Dictation slates
3) Mini-sharps

PROCEDURE : Divide the children into pairs. Give each pair a dictation slate, mini-sharps and a set of alphabet cards. One child is to set out one alphabet card, naming a particular key. The other child is to arrange the key signature on the dictation slate. Let them do this for each sharp key and then trade roles.

GAME 14—H : *CAN YOU TELL ME?*

OBJECTIVE : By this time, the children should really know how many sharps are in each key. This drill should not present any great challenge and the answers the children give should most always be correct.

MATERIALS : None

PROCEDURE : You can be the caller to first show them how the game works, but it's much more fun if the children take turns being the caller.

"I'm going to call out a letter for each of you and I want you to give me the number of sharps in that key. Let's give it a try."

"JoAnne, C."

"Zero," JoAnne answers.

"Ed, B."

"Five," answers Ed.

"Howard, A."

"Three," Howard answers, and so on around the room.

You can switch this and call out a number and let them answer back with a letter.

"Mary, two."

"D," says Mary.

For more challenge, change back and forth calling out a letter, then a number, then a letter and so on.

GAME 14–I : *MAJOR SCALES—FLATS*

OBJECTIVE : To introduce the scales containing flats — F Major, Bb Major, Eb Major, Ab Major, Db Major, Gb Major.

MATERIALS :
1) Alphabet cards — two sets, two colors
2) Blank card — same color as one set a.c.
3) Pink sharp/flat cards — use flat side
4) Alphabet person — one
5) Piano and bench

PROCEDURE : Flats can be done at the keyboard just as sharps were.

STEP ONE: Write out a C scale on the bench.
"No sharps or flats, right?"
"Right."
"Let's find the scale with one flat. For the scale with one sharp, we went up a fifth. Sharps are *up*, flats are *down*, so what shall we do to find the scale with one flat?"
"Go *down* a fifth."
"Very good!" Of course, you could go up a fourth to F, rather than down a fifth to F. However, it's less confusing and more consistant for the children to think up a fifth for sharps and down a fifth for flats.

STEP TWO: Play the F scale on the white keys.

The children will easily hear that Bb is the first flat.

Place a B card on the piano music stand.

"OK, the scale with two flats. Down a fifth to . . ."

STEP THREE: "The fifth below F is B," they'll tell you by looking at the cards and the keyboard.

Of course, you know it needs to be B♭, not B natural.

This can be explained to the children in two ways. One is that a B scale has five sharps, so it can't be the scale with two flats. The second is by ear. Play the harmonic interval of F and C (F below the C), a perfect fifth. Play the harmonic interval of B and F (B below F), a tritone. The children will hear that B♭ to F is the perfect fifth sound like F and C.

play 1st   play 2nd   play 3rd

STEP FOUR: "OK, here's the B♭ scale.[1] Let's listen for the new flat." Play the scale using only B♭ and they'll hear that E needs to be E♭. Fix the scale to read:

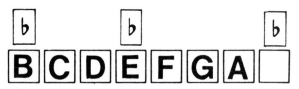

Place an E on the music stand.

STEP FIVE: "The new sharp was on what degree of the scale?"

"The fourth degree."

"Right. Do you think that the fourth degree will always be our new flat? Let's try the next scale and see if that new flat is on the fourth degree. The beginning note of the scale will be . . . "

"E♭."

---

[1] Be certain to put a flat card over the blank card, since it represents a B also.

Write a scale on E, placing the alphabet person on A, the fourth degree. Then, add the flats in order B♭, E♭.

STEP SIX: Play the scale using B♭ and the children will hear that A♭ is indeed the new flat.

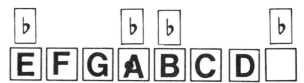

Place A on the music stand.

STEP SEVEN: You can proceed through the other flat keys in the same manner. Below are the illustrations for the completed keys.

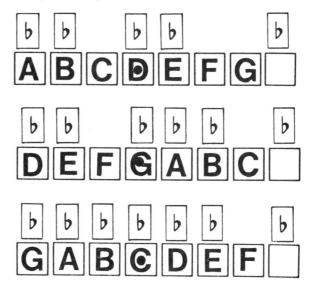

The children can memorize flats using the same games that were described for the sharps. Remembering the order of flats is easy since the children will soon notice the word "Bead". We usually just say "Bead-ga-ca" for B E A D G C.

GAME 14—J :   *I CAN WRITE ANY MAJOR SCALE YOU CAN NAME*

OBJECTIVE :   To practice sharp and flat major scales at the same time.

MATERIALS :   1) Alphabet cards
2) Blank cards
3) Alphabet people
4) Pink sharp/flat cards

PROCEDURE :   Explain that it's a very simple process to know if a certain scale contains sharps or flats. All the flat keys, except for F, have a flat in their name. So any "plain" letter other than F will be a sharp scale.

FLATS: F   B♭   E♭   A♭   D♭   G♭
SHARPS: G   D   A   E   B

Call out different letters and have the children tell you if it's a flat or sharp scale.

Explain that you're going to call out a key and you would like them to write out the scale correctly. The steps:

STEP ONE: You call out a key. Our example: "A♭ major".

STEP TWO: From the name, the children decide if it's a flat scale or a sharp scale and turn their pink sharp/flat cards so the correct accidental is facing up.

STEP THREE: They write out the scale with the alphabet and blank cards.

STEP FOUR: They place their alphabet person on the seventh degree if it's a sharp key or on the fourth degree if it's a flat key.

250

STEP FIVE: They place their sharp/flat cards on the alphabet cards stopping with the card holding the alphabet person.

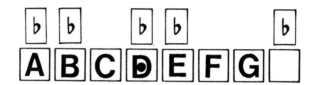

Make your directions for this game very clear before playing anything. It's important that each step be done so there's no confusion with the sharps and flats.

GAME 14—K : *KEYS IN THE MUSIC*

OBJECTIVE : To identify key signatures in the music book.

MATERIALS : Music books

PROCEDURE : Ask the children to gather around a music book you've placed on the floor. If you've a large group, try to get several copies of the music.

Just turn the pages of the music asking the children to identify the key of the piece by looking at the key signature. Point out that the key signature doesn't just appear at the beginning of the piece like the time signature, but is on the beginning of each line of music. Point out any key changes that are made using a new key signature.

It's up to you whether or not you want to discuss or ignore the fact that some of the keys will look just like major keys but will, in fact, be minor keys.

Or you can ask the children to check the beginning and ending notes and chords to see if they fit the major key signature. If they don't, you can tell them that these are probably minor keys, something they'll be studying later on.

GAME 14—L : *RELATING SCALES TO THE STRING INSTRUMENTS*

OBJECTIVE : When playing scales on the piano, it's easy to see that sharps or flats are added because a black note is substituted for a white note. On a stringed instrument, it's not quite so clear. By using the alphabet card "fingerboard", it may be easier for children to understand the concept of scales when they play. The violin will be used as the example.

MATERIALS :
1) Violins
2) Alphabet cards — five sets, five colors
3) Blank card the color of one set a.c.
4) Mini-sharps
5) Pink sharp cards
6) Alphabet people

PROCEDURE : Explain that you'd like to write out a scale with the alphabet cards first, then write it on the "fingerboard" and then play it on the violin. The first example is a C major scale.

Notice on the "fingerboard" that the cards not within the scale were turned face down so as not to confuse the child.

Next is a G major scale. First write it out with the cards as you did in WRITE A SCALE. Then you can "play" it on the "fingerboard". First turn over the cards not in use. Spell the scale out loud pointing to the cards as you do.

"G A B C D E F–sharp G."

When you come to the F-sharp, place a mini-sharp on the card and slide it up a half-step. The arrows in the drawing shows the direction the cards were moved.

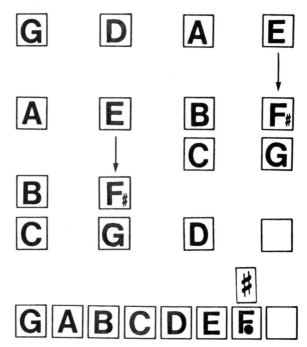

In preparation for the next scale, be certain to slide the F card back in place as you remove the mini-sharp. Continue on through the scales, playing them on the "fingerboard" as well as the real violins. Below is an example of a B major scale.

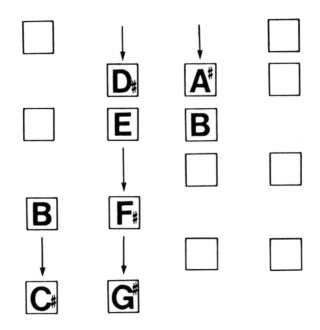

Scales using flats can be illustrated in the same manner. Just slide the cards down a half-step to form the scale. Below is an A♭ major scale.

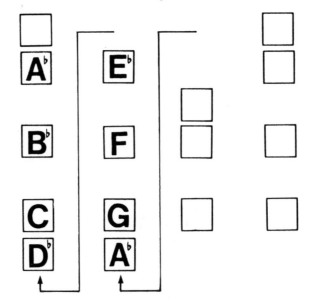

GAME 14—M : *SCALES BEFORE THE SNAKES*

OBJECTIVE : To prepare the children for two games: SCALE SNAKES and SCALES AND TRIADS. This game helps the children to think of the accidentals in sequencial order as if they were playing the scale.

MATERIALS : 1) Alphabet cards
2) Blank cards
3) Pink sharp/flat cards

PROCEDURE : Give each student a set of alphabet cards, a blank card to match, and 6 sharp/flat cards.
Call out a scale: "E Major".

STEP ONE: The children write out the scale with the alphabet cards.

STEP TWO: Then they add the sharps in order, moving left to right.

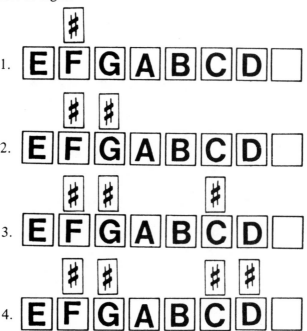

Repeat for other scales. Encourage the students to play these on their instruments.

GAME 14—N	:	*SCALE SNAKES*
OBJECTIVE	:	To have some fun with scales.
MATERIALS	:	1) Alphabet cards — many sets 2) One blank card per snake 3) Pink sharp/flat cards
PROCEDURE	:	Let the children make one snake together or if you've enough in the class or want to include parents, ask them to form three teams.

Give each group an equal number of alphabet cards, a pile of sharp/flat cards and one blank card. Explain that after you tell them the scale, you want them to write it out like a snake, putting in the accidentals *as they go along.* The blank card will be the last card on the snake.

Call out GO and away they'll go.

GAME 14—O :   *SCALES AND TRIADS*

OBJECTIVE   :   To have a good time reviewing and practicing scales, triads and key signatures. This is a board game like MUSOPOLY.

MATERIALS   :
1)   Scales and triads board
2)   Large dice
3)   Key signature cards
4)   Pink cards
5)   Play scale cards
6)   Triad cards
7)   Pennies and gold coins or other play money
8)   Alphabet people
9)   Piano or student's instrument

PROCEDURE   :   During the course of the game, children "play" scales and triads on the "keyboard" found on the board.

IN BRIEF:

As in MUSOPOLY, each child selects an alphabet person to represent him on the board. The first player rolls the dice and moves around the board in a chromatic scale.

   If he lands on a blue key (space), he's to move his

alphabet person and "play" a one-octave ascending scale beginning on that note. First, he's to say the number of sharps in the scale. If correct, he receives one penny for each sharp (or flat) used in his scale.

If the key (space) is green, the player "plays" a triad using that note as the root. Correct triads are worth two pennies.

Besides blue and green keys, there are orange, red, pink and yellow keys. When a player lands on one of these colors, he's to draw the matching color card from the center of the game board.

Orange cards:	Name the key signature shown on the card.
Red cards:	Play the scale indicated on the card on the piano or other instrument.
Yellow cards:	Identify the triad written on the card.
Pink cards:	Answer the question or do what the card says. For example: move to the Big Sharp and name all the major sharp keys. What is the key signature of two of your pieces? Play a two octave B scale.

There are other challenges and fun things to do as well. Once the children know the information needed to play it, they find it a great deal of fun.

The game is quite versatile because it can be used for any scale or triad, not just the major scales. Just imagine playing this with the Church Modes and Augmented Sixth Chords. Anyone want to join in a game?!

*Pattern for SCALES AND TRIADS is available from MUSIC 19.

GAME 14–P : *SCALE SHOW ME*

OBJECTIVE : To help the students become very fast at knowing how many sharps (or flats) are in what key.

MATERIALS : One set of alphabet cards for each player

PROCEDURE : Ask the students (and parents) to arrange themselves in a circle. Give each player one set of alphabet cards.

"Think of which scale has no sharps or flats. Take that card and place it face down in front of you." Everyone should put their C card face down.

"What scale has one sharp? Take that card and put it face down on top of your other card." G should be the card.

"Two sharps." D is the card.

"Three sharps." A is the card.

"Four sharps." E is the card.

"Five sharps is your last card." B should be placed face down on the pile.

"OK. Turn your cards over and let's say them together one at a time. C G D A E B. Very good! Next, put the extra two cards back in with the others and mix them all up. Pass your cards "up a second", or one person to your right."

After everyone has passed their cards, repeat the sequence, placing the cards face down in order of sharp scales. You can either call out the numbers—"no sharps, one sharp, two sharps, three sharps, four sharps, five sharps"—or just let them put down the cards at their own pace.

When everyone's finished, ask everyone to turn their cards face up and read through them together.

"Great. Now pass your cards 'down a third' (or skip one person and pass to your left)." Repeat the sequence several more times.

Passing the cards this way is fun to do and a good way to review intervals by pretending that each person is like a key on the piano. Once the students know their key signatures, this game is very popular.

GAMES WE PLAY CHART

O = what we plan to do

X = accomplished

Class _____

Teacher _____

Dates

Spinning the Alphabet																	
1—A What letter is this?																	
1—B Learning letters																	
1—C Fix it like mine																	
1—D Fat snake																	
1—E Fix the order																	
1—F What's missing?																	
1—G Is yours like mine?																	
1—H Pick a card																	
Make a Snake																	
2—A Snake!																	
2—B Variations on snake																	
2—C Fine																	
2—D Are these three right?																	
2—E After and before																	
2—F Phill's scrabble																	
2—G Alphabet beads																	

This Line and That Space

3—A Introducing treble clef																		
3—B Note toss I																		
3—C Introducing bass clef																		
3—D Note toss II																		
3—E Pre-bingo																		
3—F Music bingo																		
3—G Intro. the treble clef notes																		
3—H Intro. the bass clef notes																		

Blue Jello

4—A Blue jell-o																		
4—B Clap back																		
4—C Find the jellos																		
4—D Fix the jellos																		
4—E Mother, clap it																		
4—F Blue jello too-oo																		
4—G Missing blue-jello-too																		
4—H Blue pineapple jello w/ 3's and 4's																		
4—I Song fish																		

Thirds and Triads

5—A Learning thirds																		
5—B Toss down																		
5—C Fat snake																		
5—D Fix the order																		
5—E What's missing?																		
5—F Wheels																		
5—G Snake!																		

Thirds and Triads, cont.

5—H Variations on snake																	
5—I Fine																	
5—J Pick a card																	
5—K After and before																	
5—L Are these triads right?																	
5—M Win a triad I																	
5—N Win a triad II																	
5—O Thirds scrabble																	
5—P Show me																	
5—Q Interval circle																	

Lines or Spaces

6—A Lines—treble clef																	
6—B Hand staff																	
6—C Toss																	
6—D Pass out																	
6—E What note is missing?																	
6—F Anything wrong?																	
6—G In this order																	
6—H Spaces—treble clef																	

One Clef

7—A Pick a pair																	
7—B Pass out																	
7—C Fix one																	
7—D Mother, fix it																	
7—E What's right?																	

One Clef, cont.																	
7–F Introducing staff cards																	
7–G Match this card																	
7–H Match this card—backwards																	
7–I Line 'em up																	
7–J Use 'em up																	
7–K Bingo with names																	
7–L Toss																	
7–M Show me with names																	
7–N Relay																	
7–O I can name it																	
7–P Name it																	
7–Q Pairs with slates																	
7–R Staff card snakes																	
7–S No clef																	
7–T Lines—bass clef																	
7–U Spaces—bass clef																	
7–V Lines and spaces—bass clef																	
7–W Name that note																	
Signs and Symbols																	
8–A Dynamics																	
8–B Dynamic mix-up																	
8–C Crescendo and decrescendo																	
8–D Follow that sign																	
8–E Sharps and flats																	
8–F Learning the others																	
8–G Pass around and act out																	
8–H What can you find?																	
8–I I see																	
8–J The big pyramid																	

Signs and Symbols, cont.

8–K What can you hear?																
8–L Match a symbol																
8–M Learning tempos																
8–N Tempo mix-up																
8–O Tempo pass out																
8–P Tempos in the music																

Musopoly

9–A Musopoly																

Play It Again—Dictation

10–A Introducing dictation																
10–B Dictation with numbers																
10–C Dictation with notes																
10–D Put your finger on it																
10–E Hear any thirds?																
10–F Write mine																
10–G More numbers																
10–H Heard this before?																
10–I Major or minor																
10–J Three intervals																
10–K Chicken soup																
10–L Interval circle dictation																
10–M Song puzzle snakes																
10–N Song puzzle pass out																

Name That Note

11−A Match this card																		
11−B Match this card —backwards																		
11−C Line'em up																		
11−D Show me with names																		
11−E Name it																		
11−F I can name it																		
11−G Keep on matching																		
11−H Name that note																		
11−I Staff card pairs																		
11−J Staff card teams																		
11−K Fish																		
11−L Octave pairs																		
11−M Bingo−both clefs																		
11−N Not really triads																		
11−O Super snake																		
11−P Ledger line staff cards																		

The Long and the Short

12−A Real rhythms																		
12−B Making change																		
12−C Dotted rhythms																		
12−D Rest, rest, rest																		
12−E Write a song																		
12−F What song is this?																		
12−G Guess my song																		
12−H Teaching 3/4 time																		
12−I Rhythm card snakes																		
12−J Rhythm mix-up																		
12−K Rhythm song snakes																		

The Long and the Short, cont.																	
12—L Knee slappers																	
12—M Teaching other meters																	
12—N Duple, triple or quadruple																	
12—O Notes and rests																	
Snakes and People on the Piano																	
13—A Three fingers—two fingers																	
13—B People on the piano																	
13—C This note and that key																	
13—D Natural half-steps bc and ef																	
13—E Line up a keyboard																	
13—F Staff and "keyboard"																	
13—G Keyboard relay																	
13—H High and low																	
13—I Place the people																	
13—J Toss, name, and find it																	
13—K Staff cards and the "keyboard"																	
13—L I'm a string player																	
13—M Find this note																	
Scales and Key Signatures																	
14—A Major scales—sharps																	
14—B F C G D A																	
14—C Write a scale—sharps																	
14—D Fix the sharps																	
14—E Key signatures—sharps																	
14—F I know my key signatures																	

Scales and Key Signatures, cont.

14–G Key signature pairs																	
14–H Can you tell me?																	
14–I Major scales—flats																	
14–J I can write any major scale you can name																	
14–K Keys in music																	
14–L Relating scales to the string instruments																	
14–M Scales before the snakes																	
14–N Scale snakes																	
14–O Scales and triads brd. gm.																	
14–P Scale show me																	

DESCRIPTION OF MATERIALS

1. **ALPHABET CARDS**

2. **ONE-STAFF BOARD AND CLEFS**

3. **TWO-STAFF BOARD AND CLEFS**

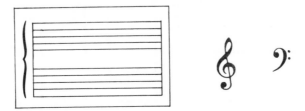

4. **TOSS NOTE**

5. **LEDGER LINE SHEET**

clear plastic

6. **BINGO CARDS AND DOTS**

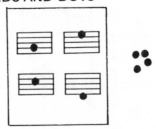

7. BLUE JELLO STICKS AND "TWO" RINGS

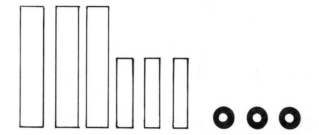

8. ORANGE (SYMBOL) CARDS

9. WORD CARDS

10. NOTES WITH LETTERS

11. BASS AND TREBLE STAFF CARDS

12. DICTATION SLATES

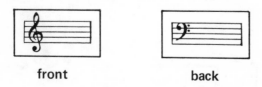

front   back

13. NUMBER SLATES

14. LEDGER LINE STAFF CARDS

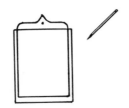

15. RHYTHM CARDS

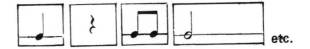

etc.

16. RHYTHM BOARDS

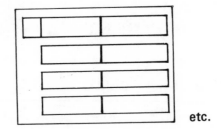

etc.

17. PINK SHARP/FLAT CARDS

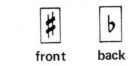

front   back

18. BLANK CARDS

19. MINI-SHARPS AND MINI-FLATS

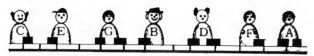

clear plastic

20. FELT SHARPS AND FELT FLATS

♯ ♭

21. ALPHABET PEOPLE

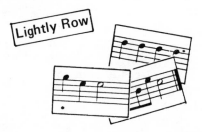

22. SONG PUZZLE CARDS

23. YELLOW TEMPO CARDS

Lento

Presto

INDEX OF GAMES